The Black Book of
VILLAINS

The Black Book of V

Printed in Great Britain
for David & Charles (Publishers) Limited.
Brunel House Newton Abbot Devon

Design: Vic Giolitto

ISBN 0 7153 7030 8

4 **Introduction**
6 **Alberich** The Rhinegold/Richard Wagner
9 **Carver Doone** Lorna Doone/R. D. Blackmore
12 **Bluebeard** Contes du Temps Passé de ma Mère L'oie/Charles Perrault
15 **Bluto** Popeye/Elzie Crisler Segar
16 **Napoleon the Pig** Animal Farm/George Orwell
18 **Moriarty** Sherlock Holmes/Conan Doyle
21 **Cain** The Bible
23 **Godfrey Ablewhite** The Moonstone/Wilkie Collins
25 **Bill Sikes** Oliver Twist/Charles Dickens
28 **Captain Hook** Peter and Wendy/James Barrie
31 **Chauvelin** Scarlet Pimpernel/Baroness Orczy
34 **Count Dracula** Dracula/Bram Stoker
38 **Dom Claude Frollo** The Hunchback of Notre Dame/Victor Hugo
41 **Cruella De Vil** The Hundred and One Dalmatians/Dodie Smith
43 **Dorian Gray** The Picture of Dorian Gray/Oscar Wilde
46 **Edward Hyde** The Strange Case of Dr Jekyll and Mr Hyde/Robert Louis Stevenson
50 **Goldfinger** Goldfinger/Ian Fleming
52 **Fu Manchu**/Sax Rohmer
56 **Carl Peterson** Bulldog Drummond/Sapper
58 **Peter Quint** The Turn of the Screw/Henry James

LLAINS

Janet Pate

David & Charles London/Newton Abbot

60 **The Marquis de St. Evremonde** A Tale of Two Cities/Charles Dickens
64 **Injun Joe** The Adventures of Tom Sawyer/Mark Twain
67 **The Joker** Batman
70 **Lady Macbeth** Macbeth/William Shakespeare
75 **Long John Silver** Treasure Island/Robert Louis Stevenson
78 **Hindley Earnshaw** Wuthering Heights/Emily Brontë
82 **Brian de Bois Guilbert** Ivanhoe/Sir Walter Scott
85 **Mr Grimes** The Water Babies/Charles Kingsley
87 **Mrs Danvers** Rebecca/Daphne du Maurier
90 **Brer Fox** Uncle Remus/Noel Chandler Harris
92 **Harry Flashman** Tom Brown's Schooldays/Thomas Hughes
94 **Polyphemus the Cyclops** The Odyssey/Homer
97 **Squire Thornhill** The Vicar of Wakefield/Oliver Goldsmith
100 **Rupert of Hentzau** The Prisoner of Zenda/Anthony Hope
103 **The Sheriff of Nottingham** The Legend of Robin Hood/Folklore
106 **Simon Legree** Uncle Tom's Cabin/Harriet Beecher Stowe
108 **Sir Percival Glyde** The Woman in White/Wilkie Collins
110 **Sweeney Todd** The String of Pearls/Thomas Preskett Prest
112 **Svengali** Trilby/George du Maurier
116 **Uriah Heep** David Copperfield/Charles Dickens
120 **Acknowledgements**

Introduction

This book is not a comprehensive study of villainy but an anthology of villainous characters. It can be read through or dipped into. Each villain has his own section which includes a short biography, a quotation from the author's or inventor's source and some background notes. These vary in content with each villain, from a short study of Queen Gruoch (the real Lady Macbeth) to a speech delivered by Mr James Barrie on Captain Hook's days as a schoolboy at Eton, and the extraordinary life story of Mr Charles Perrot, the character of Bluebeard, a seventeenth-century villain with enough violence in

him to compete with most modern horror characters. All the villains are fictitious, although some have their roots in fact. The Sheriff of Nottingham, Dracula and Lady Macbeth are all characters based on history. Carver Doone is part of the famous west-country legend of the Doones of Exmoor, which evidence shows to have at least some basis in fact. Alberich from Wagner's Ring cycle and the Cyclops Polyphemus from Homer's *Odyssey* are both mythological. Injun Joe, Uriah Heep and Flashman all come from works that are largely biographical: *Tom Sawyer, David Copperfield* and *Tom Brown's School Days*. Certainly Injun Joe existed and that really was his name. The original was not as bad as Mark Twain's character, though,

Lyn Harding as Sikes in the 1905 stage version of *Oliver Twist* at His Majesty's Theatre, London.

John Barrymore as Svengali and Marian Marsh as Trilby in the 1931 screen version of *Svengali*.

in fact, not bad at all, but a sad old man who died an alcoholic. Bluto and The Joker are villains of the comic strip and cartoon film. It was difficult choosing these two from a wealth of comic-book villainy. In the end, Bluto had to be included because he is such a wholehearted baddy, his villainy is simple and basic. Also he passes one of the acid tests—he enjoys his work. Neither Frankenstein nor his monster are included because, unlike the others, they are not intentional villains, victims of circumstance. Edward Hyde and Count Dracula fill the monster's gap, and the supernatural is

'covered' by Peter Quint (from *The Turn of the Screw* by Henry James) and Dorian Gray (from *The Picture of Dorian Gray* by Oscar Wilde). It is interesting to compare the villainy of Carl Peterson (from *Bulldog Drummond* by Sapper), Moriarty (from *Sherlock Holmes* by Arthur Conan Doyle) and Goldfinger (from *Goldfinger* by Ian Fleming). Although these are products of different periods, their similarity is striking.

All the villains in this book are classics in their own right, created by such masters of their craft as Charles Dickens, Victor Hugo, Mark Twain, Sir Walter Scott, etc—not to mention Shakespeare and Homer. A fact which emerged while I was researching the products of these fertile minds was that all their villains are three-dimensional. I cannot help liking them in one way or another. I shall miss working with them, but I shall go on reading them. Life would be dull without them.

Captain Hook in the Walt Disney 1952 screen version of *Peter Pan*.

Max Schrek as Dracula in the 1922 screen version of *Nosferatu*.

Alberich

From **The Rhinegold** By **Richard Wagner**

'Presently there comes a poor devil of a dwarf stealing along the slippery rocks of the river bed, a creature with energy enough to make him strong of body and fierce of passion, but with a brutish narrowness of intelligence and selfishness of imagination; too stupid to see that his own welfare can only be compassed as part of the welfare of the world, too full of brute force not to grab vigorously at his own gain. Such dwarfs are common in London. . . . He comes now with a fruitful impulse in him, in search of what he lacks in himself, beauty, lightness of heart, imagination, music. The Rhine maidens, representing all these to him, fill him with hope and longing; and he never considers that he has nothing to offer that they could possibly desire being by natural limitation incapable of seeing anything from anyone else's point of view. With perfect simplicity, he offers himself as a sweetheart to them. . . .

'They mock him atrociously, pretending to fall in love with him at first sight, and then slipping away and making game of him, heaping ridicule and disgust on the poor wretch until he is beside himself with mortification and rage. They forget him when the water begins to glitter in the sun, and the gold to reflect its glory . . . and though they know the parable of Klondyke quite well, they have no fear that the gold will be wrenched away by the dwarf, since it will yield to no one who has not forsaken love for it. . . .

'He forswears love as thousands of us forswear it every day; and in a moment the gold is in his grasp, and he disappears in the depths, leaving the water fairies vainly screaming "Stop thief"! whilst the river seems to plunge into darkness and sink from us as we rise to the cloud regions above. . . .'

Bernard Shaw The Perfect Wagnerite

The Story

The Rhinemaidens are the guardians of the Rhinegold, the golden treasure that lies at the bottom of the river Rhine. If he who possesses it renounces love he will become the ruler of the world.
The dwarf Alberich emerges from the underground kingdom of the Nibelungs and begins to flirt with the Rhinemaidens who guard the Rhinegold. They laugh at him, but in their teasing disclose the secret of the power of the Rhinegold. Angry at their rejection of him Alberich is only too eager to renounce love for the power that the gold will bring him. He snatches the gold and carries it away to his underground world. Here he forges a helmet and ring of gold and becomes the ruler of the Nibelungs. The golden helmet which is fashioned by his brother Mime from the Rhinegold renders the wearer invisible, and able to assume any shape he wishes.

Wotan, King of the gods, comes with his brother, Loge, god of fire and deceit, to the caverns of the Nibelung, to steal the Rhinegold. He plans to give the gold to the giants Fasolt and Fafner as payment for their building of Valhalla, the new home of the gods. They have demanded Friea, the goddess of youth, as payment for their work, but Wotan and Loge are certain that the giants will accept the gold in her stead. Loge persuades Alberich to demonstrate the powers of the Tarnhelm, the magic helmet of gold. Alberich turns himself into a toad, and is immediately seized by Loge and Wotan. Reluctantly he is made to give up the Rhinegold, but he places a curse on all future possessors of the Ring. The curse begins to work as soon as the giants receive the Rhinegold as payment from Wotan. They fight, and Fafner slays Fasolt.

After many adventures in which Wotan tries unsuccessfully to return the Rhinegold to the Rhinemaidens, Alberich's revenge is completed when the gods are led to self destruction through the pursuit of the Ring.

The Background

The dwarfs of mythology were said to be found working in mines. As their skills in mining were greater than man's they were looked upon as the rightful guardians of buried treasure. They were skilful goldsmiths and made weapons and jewellery for the Gods and Goddesses.

Wagner found the character of Alberich the dwarf in the folklore of Germany and in the Norse sagas. According to the German legend Alberich (Elfrich, Aelfric) guards the treasure belonging to the Nibelung king. Siegfried vanquishes Alberich and seizes the treasure.

The Norse dwarf is Andvari, able to change himself into a fish and live in the water. He is captured by Loki in a magic net and given his freedom in exchange for the treasure. He attempts to withold the ring which has the power to create more treasure. But Loki sees the Ring and forces it from him. Andvari curses the Ring and the Gold, and swears that whoever possesses them will be destroyed. The curse is fulfilled. Loki is killed by his son Fafnir for the possession of the gold, and is in turn slain by Sigurd.

Arthur Rackham's interpretation of Alberich from *The Ring of the Nibelungen* published in 1910.

In the theatre

Götterdämmerung (The Twilight of the Gods)

1876   Bayreuth Festival Theatre
First performance 17 August

1879   Vienna Opera House
First performance abroad 14 February

1888   New York
First performance in America 25 January
Sung in German

The Ring Cycle of the Four Operas

1876   Bayreuth Festival
First performance 13–17 August

A nineteenth-century painting by Joseph Hoffman of the 1876 Bayreuth production of *Das Rheingold*.

1879   Vienna Opera House
First performance abroad 26–30 May

1882   Her Majesty's Theatre (London)
First performance in England 5–9 May

1889   New York
4–11 March

Das Rheingold (The Rhinegold)

1869   Munich Court Opera House
First performance 22 September

1878   Vienna Opera House
First performance abroad 24 January

1889   New York
First performance in America 4 January
Sung in German

Die Walkure (The Valkyrie)

1870   Munich Court Opera House
First performance 26 June

1877   Vienna Opera House
First performance abroad 5 March

1877   New York
First performance in America 2 April

1895   Covent Garden Opera House (England)
First performance in England 16 October
Translation by H. F. Corder

Siegfried

1876   Bayreuth Festival Theatre
First performance 16 August

1878   Vienna Opera House
First performance abroad 9 November

1887   New York
First performance in America 9 November
Sung in German

1901   Manchester
First performance in England 18 October
Translated by H. F. Corder

Alberich in print

Der Ring des Nibelungen (privately printed Zürich, 1853)

1877   *The Nibelung's Ring*, English words by
A. Forman

1822   H. F. Corder (Mainz)

1896   Schott & Co (London), translation by
F. Jameson

1899– Longman's and Co, translated by R. Rankin.
1901 Two volumes

1909   *Ring of the Nibelung* by Alice L. Cleatham
(an interpretation embodying Wagner's own
explanation)

1910   Translated by Margaret Armour, illustrated
by Arthur Rackham

1913   Smith, Elder & Co (London), translated by
Randle Fynes

1913   Bridtkopf & Hartel (London), translated by
Ernest Newman

Carver Doone

From **Lorna Doone** By **R. D. Blackmore**

A nineteenth-century painting by C. E. Brook of Carver Doone.

'. . . I became aware of a great man coming leisurely down the valley. He had a broad brimmed hat, and a leather jerkin and heavy jack boots to his middle thigh, and what was worst of all for me, on his shoulder he bore a long carbine.

'. . . Presently the great man re-appeared . . . and though I am not a judge of men's faces, there was something in his which turned me cold, as though with a kind of horror. Not that it was an ugly face; nay, rather it seemed a handsome one, so far as mere form and line might go, full of strength and vigour, and will, and steadfast resolution.

From the short black hair above the broad forehead, to the long black beard descending below the curt bold chin, there was not any curve, or glimpse of weakness, or of afterthought. Nothing playful, nothing pleasant, nothing with a track for smiles; nothing which a friend could like, and laugh at him for having. . . .

'And yet he might have been a good man. . . .

'I say that he might have seemed a good man . . . but for the cold and cruel hankering of his steel blue eyes. . . .'
R. D. Blackmore

The Story

There are many legends surrounding the Doones of Exmoor. Certainly a band of brigands does seem to have terrorised North Devon during the seventeenth century. Stories of their origin vary. Were they men of high rank who lost their homes during the Civil War and turned to lawlessness? Is the word Doone a North Devon corruption of Dane, the dreaded invader? Were Doones the Welsh clan Dwn (pronounced Doone) who inter-married with the neighbouring Ryd family? The most romantic (and therefore let us hope the true) tale compares favourably with historical fact. A family feud existed between Sir James Stuart Doune, who assumed the Earldom of Moray through his marriage, and his twin brother, Endor, over the title and estates of Doune Castle. James was murdered in 1602 by the Earl of Huntley, but it was generally supposed that Huntley was in the pay of Ensor. James was succeeded by his son who was reconciled to Huntley. After Ensor's death his son continued the family feud, assuming the surname of Doune. Seeing this as a claim on Doune Castle, his cousin attacked him and his wife, Margaret MacGregor, at their home in Stirling, and drove them out of Scotland. Ensor, (now Sir) and Lady Doune went to London to seek redress from the King. Failing this they made their way to the remote West Country, to isolate themselves from the world. They settled in Exmoor and their sons were brought up to think of all men as their enemies. They terrorised the neighbourhood with their violent crimes. In 1699, the Earl of Moray being dead, his grandson offered the Dounes a peaceful return and compensation for the wrongs suffered by them.

The Background

Carver is the eldest son of Ensor Doone, an embittered Scottish nobleman, who, robbed of his inheritance, settled with his family and followers in a remote part of North Devon. Their terrorisation of the neighbourhood makes them feared and hated by the local people. On the death of his father, Carver, a cruel giant of a man, becomes the leader of the Doones. He has been promised marriage to Lorna Doone, who was kidnapped as a child by the Doones and brought up as one of them. Lorna falls in love with John Ridd, a local farmer, who carries her off to live with his family. Carver tries unsuccessfully to recapture her.

The local people, no longer able to endure the Doones' terrorisation of them, attack and destroy their settlement. Only Carver and Counsellor Doone escape. Hearing that John and Lorna are to be married, Carver goes to the Church and shoots Lorna as she stands at the altar. John pursues him and after a furious fight Carver falls into the black mud of the moor and is sucked down to his death. Lorna survives, and she and John live a happily married life together.

Lorna Doone on film

Silents

1912 Clarendon Film Production
Director Wilfred Noy

1915 Biograph Company

1920 Lucoque Ltd/Butchers Films

1922 First National
Director Maurice Tournier
Carver (Donald Macdonald)

Sound

1934 Basil Dean Production
Carver (Roy Emmerson)

1951 Columbia Pictures
Ridd (Richard Greene)
Carver (William Bishop)

1963 BBC Television Production
Carver (Andrew Faulds)

Above: A scene from the 1951 screen version of *Lorna Doone* and below: the 1934 version.

Lorna Doone in print

(*A selected list*)

1869   Sampson Low & Co (London), **3** volumes

1875   Harper & Bros (New York)

1883   Sampson Low & Co (London), illustrated by Mr W. Small & Mr W. H. J. Boot, introduction and notes by H. Sowden Ward

1908   Sampson Low Marston & Co (London), landscapes by Charles E. Brittan, Figure subjects by Charles E. Brock

1911   Sampson Low & Co (London), abridged and edited for schools by Wm. A. Warren

1911   Macmillan's Pocket American and English Classics, edited with introduction and notes by Albert L. Barbour

1913   Nelson's Classics (London)

1914   Oxford University Press (Oxford), introduction by T. Herbert Warren

1920   G. G. Harrap & Co. (London), printed in the USA, illustrated by Rowland Wheelwright-William Sewell

1933   *Daily Express* Publications

1937   T. Nelson & Sons (London), illustrated by A. M. Trotter

1948   Geo. G. Harrap & Co (London), Sword in Hand Library, retold by Hayden Peny (with map and glossary)

1950   Macdonald (London), Macdonald Illustrated Classics

1961   Frederick Warne & Co (London and New York), abridged edition, illustrated by Norman Buchanan

1966   Dent (London), Dutton (New York), introduction by R. L. Blackmore

1970   Collins (London), abridged by Olive Jones, illustrated by Pauline Baynes

Bluebeard

From **Contes Du Temps Passé De Ma Mere
L'oie** By **Charles Perrault**
(Tales of Past Times by Mother Goose)

Pierre Brasseur as Bluebeard
in the 1951 screen version
Barbe Bleu.

'Il estoit une fois un homme qui avoit de belles maisons a la Ville et a la Campagne, de la vaisselle d'or & d'argent des meubles en broderie, et des carosses tout dorés; mais par malheur cet homme avoit la Barbe-bleue: cela le rendoit si laid et si terrible, qu'l n'estoit ni femme ni fille qui ne s'enfuit de devant luy.'
Charles Perrault

There was a man who had fine houses, both in town and country, a deal of silver and gold plate, embroidered furniture, and coaches gilded all over with gold. But this man had the misfortune to have a Blue beard, which made him so frightfully ugly, that all the women and girls ran away from him.
Translated by R. S. Gent

The Story

Bluebeard brings his new bride, Fatima, to his rich home. When business takes him away he leaves her with all the keys of the house, telling her she may go wherever she likes—except into the Blue Closet. Her curiosity aroused, Fatima goes to the closet. Inside she finds the murdered, headless corpses of Bluebeard's previous wives. In her panic she drops the key of the closet into a pool of blood and all her efforts to clean it are to no avail. The key is enchanted and as fast as she cleans one side the blood stain appears on the other. When Bluebeard sees the key he prepares to behead her. But she is saved by the timely arrival of her two soldier brothers who fight and kill him.

The moral

Moralité
La curiosité malgré tous ses attraits,
  Couste souvent bien des regrets;
On en voit tous les jours mille exemples paroistre,
C'est, n'en deplaise au sexe, un plaisir bien leger,
  Des qu'on le prend il cesse d'estre,
  Et toujours il couste trop cher.
Perrault

O curiosity, thou mortal bane,
Spite of thy charms, thou causest often pain
And sore regret, of which we daily find
A thousand instances attend mankind:
For thou, O may it not displease the fair,
A flitting pleasure art, but lasting care:
And always costs, alas! too dear the prize,
Which, in the moment of possession, dies.
Translated by R. S. Gent

A drawing of a scene from the *Extravaganza* by H. B. Farnie at the Charing Cross Theatre, London.

Autre Moralite
Pour peu qu'on ait l'esprit sensé,
Et que du Monde on scache le grimoire,
On voit bien-tost que cette histoire
Est un conte du temps passé;
Il n'est plus d'epoux si terrible,
Ny qui demande l'impossible;
Fut-il mal-content & jaloux,
Pres de sa femme on le voit filer doux;
Et de quelque couleur que sa barbe puisse estre,
On a peine a juger qui des deux est le maistre.
Charles Perrault

A very little share of common sense,
And knowledge of the world, will soon evince,
That this a story is of time long pass'd,
No husbands now such panic terrors cast;
Nor weakly, with a vain despotic hand,
Imperious, what's impossible, command;
And they discontented, or the fire
Of wicked jealousy their hearts inspire,
They softly sing; and of whatever hue
Their beards may chance to be, or black, or blue,
Grizeld or suffet, it is hard to say,
Which of the two, the man or wife, bears sway.
Translated by R. S. Gent

The Background

From an early age, Charles Perrault, born in Paris on 12 January 1628, showed he had an original mind. Finding school too formal an institution for the development of his young mind, he and his friend, Beaurin, left and superintended their own studies in the Luxembourg gardens for three or four years. In 1651 he obtained a degree—in Orleans where they were notoriously easy to come by—and was called to the Bar. After tiring of the law he worked for one of his brothers who was Receiver-General of Paris. He must go on record as

one of the most gifted amateurs of all time, for without any previous training, he turned his hand to architecture (in 1663 his efforts earned him a post as Assistant Superintendant of the Royal buildings under Colbert, the Finance Minister), invention (he introduced election by ballot to the Academy of Medals and Inscriptions and invented a ballot machine), writer of commemorative verse (this commission from Colbert at a fee of, eventually, 1000 livres a year, lasted for twenty years). He designed tapestries. His first book was a burlesque of the Sixth Book of Aeneid. A reading of his anti-classical poem, *Le Siecle de Louis XIV*, in which he stated that Homer would have been a far better poet had he been born in the reign of Louis XIV, was the start of a ten-year battle of words. The poet Boileau claimed that Perrault had insulted the great men of the past, he wrote ferocious epigrams about Perrault and denounced his ignorance of Latin and Greek. Perrault remained calm and wrote a comedy, *L'Oublieux'*, in which he satirised people who 'publish old books with a great many notes'. Perrault's fairy tales were not written until he was nearly seventy. The first collection was published in 1697, under the name of his son, P. Darmancour. A lasting memorial to Perrault are the Tuileries gardens, which, while working for Colbert, he saved from becoming exclusively for Royal use. He said, 'I am persuaded that the gardens of Kings are made so great and spacious that all their children may walk in them'.

Bluebeard on film

Silent

1902   The Warwick Trading Company
        (Short sequence showing Dan Leno starring
        in Drury Lane Pantomime Production)

1914   *Bluebeard the Second* (Biograph)

1914   Ambrosio Production Co, Italy
        Bluebeard's Chamber

Sound

1938   Clay puppet film by Rene Bertrand
        (The original Perrault Mother Goose story)

1945   Pathe / International
        Bluebeard
        Starring John Carradine
        (Jack the Ripper type murder story set in
        Paris in the 1890s)

1951   Alcina Production Co
        Barbe Bleu
        Starring Pierre Brasseur

1964   Norman Foster Production
        Bluebeard's Castle
        (Television Film based on Bartok's Opera)

14

Bluebeard in the theatre

1791   Pantomime
        Covent Garden Theatre

1874   Extravaganza by H. B. Farnie
        Charing Cross Theatre

Bluebeard in print

A selected list

Barbe Bleu (Bluebeard) is taken from *Contes Des Fées* (Fairy Tales) by Charles Perrault. First published in 1697 in Volume 5, Part 4, of *Moetjens Recueil*

1697   *Contes Des Fées. Histoire Du Contes Du Temps
        Passé.
        Avec des Muralitez Par Le Fils*

1724   New edition
        Other editions followed in 1781, 1836, 1861,
        1864, and 1875

1729   Pub. J. Pote. Translated into English by
        Mr Samber

1791   T. Cadell (London)
        *The airs, glees, choruses in the new Pantomime
        of Bluebeard*

1810   *The History of Bluebeard, or the fatal effects of
        Curiosity and Disobedience.* J. Pitts (London)

1861   *Bluebeard.* J. Bysh (London)

1862   *Dessins par Gustave Doré.* J. Bysh (Paris)

1870   *Bluebeard* Dean & Son (London), illustrated

1880   *Barbe Bleu. Les Conte De Perrault.*
        (Tradut en Arabe Useul De L'Agerie.)
        Par M. Tibal (Alger)

1888   *Perrault's Popular Tales.* Clarendon Press
        (Oxford)
        (edited from the original editions by
        Andrew Lang)

1897   *The Fairy Tales of Master Perrault.* Pitt Press
        Series

1895   *The Story of Bluebeard from Perrault.*
        Lawrence and Bullen (London), illustrated
        with pictures and ornaments by J. E. Southall

1909   *Contes Des Fées*
        (La Barbe Bleu—Le Petit Chaperon Rouge—
        Piquet a la Houppe—Peau D'Ane)
        (Siepmann's French Series for Rapid Reading)
        Macmillan and Co (London)

1957   Penguin Classics. (Harmondsworth)
        Translated with an introduction by Geoffrey
        Brereton.

1961   Kingfisher Colour Book.
        Ward Lock and Co (London)

1960   *The authentic Mother Goose Fairy Tales and
        Nursery Rhymes*
        Edited by Jacques Barchilon and Henry Pettit,
        containing a photographic reprint enlarged
        of Perrault's 'Histories or Tales of Past
        Times'. Published in London 1729
        Published Alan Swallow (Denver)

1967   *Perrault's Fairy Tales.* Jonathan Cape
        (London), translated by Anne Carter,
        illustrated by Janus Grabianski

1969   Dover Publications (New York),
        translated A. E. Johnson, illustrated Gustav
        Doré.

Bluto

From **Popeye** By **Elzie Crisler Segar**

Bluto is mean and burly. His aim in life to carry off the delectable Olive Oyl and make her his own, is constantly thwarted by her sweetheart, Popeye the sailor man. Although a classically natural, winner-take-all, dirty fighter, Bluto is continually at a disadvantage when faced with Popeye, who, whenever he finds himself in a tight spot, simply downs a tin of Spinach. The Spinach acts as an instant energy and muscle builder, enabling him to perform feats of strength to which the hapless Bluto is quite unequal. (A statue to Popeye, erected in 1937, stands in Crystal City, Texas. Heart of the spinach growing country.)

The Background

Olive Oyl's family dates back to 'The Thimble Theatre' drawn in 1919 by Elzie Crisler Segar. They were joined in 1929 by Popeye the Sailor man, whose main problem in those days was avoiding Olive Oyl's matrimonial plans. Bluto made his first appearance in a comic strip dated 14 June 1933, in a story called 'The Eighth Sea'. In the early 1960s King Features produced a series of cartoons for television, in which Bluto was renamed Brutus.

During the war Mussolini banned all American cartoon strips in Italy, but public demand for Popeye and Bluto was so great that they were allowed to remain.

When Elzie Crisler Segar died, the Popeye comic strip was continued first by Bela Zaboly, who in turn was succeeded by Ralph Stern and in turn by Bud Sagendorf.

Popeye on film

Paramount

	Animator:
1933	Max Fleischer
1940	Dave Fleischer
1947	Seymour Kneitel
1948	Bill Tytla
1950	Seymour Kneitel
1952	I. Sparber
1953	Seymour Kneitel
1954	I. Sparber

Popeye has not been produced on the stage.

Napoleon the Pig

From **Animal Farm** By **George Orwell**

'Napoleon was a large, rather fierce-looking Berkshire boar, the only Berkshire on the farm, not much of a talker, but with a reputation for getting his own way.'
George Orwell

An illustration by Halas and Batchelor of the Pig Napoleon from the 1954 edition of *Animal Farm*.

The Story

One of the leaders of the successful animal rebellion on Manor Farm against man's subjection of the animals for his own gain, Napoleon, gradually and with cruel ruthlessness, takes over the leadership of the new regime and replaces the hard-won ideals ('All animals are equal') with his own despotism ('But some animals are more equal than others'). The betrayal of the animals is complete when Napoleon and the other pigs stand up on two legs and fraternise with man. The exploitation of the animals by the pigs becomes as ruthless as their previous exploitation by man. There is no difference now—between pig and man.

Animal Farm was written between November 1943 and February 1944. 'The only one of my books', wrote Orwell, 'that I really sweated over'. It was rejected by several publishers, fortuitously, as it turned out, for Secker & Warburg accepted it in 1945, when its publication coincided with the German surrender and the subsequent disillusionment with the Soviet Union.

The film version changed the ending of Orwell's original story: the animals all over the world rise up and expel Napoleon, and bring peace to the animal kingdom. A happy ending which completely detracted from the author's original and ominous message.

Animal Farm on film

1954 Halas and Batchelor full-length feature cartoon
Distributed by Anglo/EMI
(The narration and all the voices of the
animals by Maurice Denham)

**The Pig Napoleon from the 1954 full-length cartoon
screen version of *Animal Farm*.**

Animal Farm in print

(*A selected list*)

1945 Secker & Warburg (London)

1946 Harcourt, Brace & Co (New York)

1951 Penguin (Harmondsworth)

1954 Secker & Warburg (London), illustrated by
Joy Batchelor and John Halas

1954 Longmans (London)

1960 Longmans (London), introduction and notes
by Laurence Brandon

Moriarty

From **Sherlock Holmes** By **Sir Arthur Conan Doyle**

'He is extremely tall and thin, his forehead domes out in a white curve, and his two eyes are deeply sunken in his head. He is clean shaven, pale, and ascetic looking, retaining something of the professor in his features. His shoulders are rounded from much study, and his face protrudes forward and is for ever slowly oscillating from side to side in a curiously reptilian fashion. . . .

'. . . the man pervades London, and no one has heard of him. That's what puts him on a pinnacle in the records of crime. I tell you, Watson, in all seriousness, that if I could beat that man, if I could free society of him, I should feel that my own career had reached its summit; and I should be prepared to turn to some more placid line in life. . .'
Sir Arthur Conan Doyle

The Story

At the age of 21 Moriarty wrote a treatise on the Binominal Theorem. It won him a mathematical chair at a small university. Compelled to resign his chair through rumours of his criminal leanings, he came to London as an Army coach. He was soon in control of a complicated criminal network unsuspected by all save Sherlock Holmes. Their battle of wits eventually takes them to Switzerland and the brink of the Reichenbach Falls, where, on 4 May 1891, after a life and death struggle, they both appear to have fallen to their deaths. But, in the spring of 1894, Holmes re-appears and tells how, using his knowledge of Japanese wrestling, he had struggled free of Moriarty's grip and watched his death fall.

An illustration of Professor Moriarty by Sidney Paget from the 1893 edition of the *Strand Magazine*.

An illustration of the death of
Sherlock Holmes and
Moriarty by Sidney Paget
from the 1893 edition of the
Strand Magazine.

The Background

The first Sherlock Holmes story was bought by Ward Locke & Co for £25 and published at the end of 1887 in *Beeton's Christmas Annual*. Later the 'Strand' magazine serialised the stories and they were collected into separate volumes between 1891 and 1927. In 1893 Conan Doyle grew tired of Holmes and created Moriarty to 'kill him off'.

Public outcry was immediate and overwhelming. Doyle received thousands of protesting letters and in London young men wore black crepe in their hats.

At this time Doyle found such intense public reaction to the death of his fictitious character cruelly ironic, as he had just learned of the imminent death of his wife from tuberculosis.

In 1901, after much pressure from all sides, he was forced to resurrect Holmes. It has been alleged that Moriarty was based on Sigmund Freud, who was staying in the same Swiss hotel as Doyle when *The Final Problem* was written.

Gustav von Seyffertitz as Moriarty and John Barrymore as Sherlock Holmes in the 1922 screen version of *Sherlock Holmes*.

Sherlock Holmes on film

1916 Essanay
      Sherlock Holmes
      (Film version of the William Gillette play)

1922 Goldwyn Films
      Sherlock Holmes
      Moriarty (Gustav Von Seyffertitz)

1929 Paramount
      The Return of Sherlock Holmes
      Moriarty (Harry T. Morey)

1930 First Division Films
      The Sleeping Cardinal (or *Sherlock Holmes Fatal Hour*)
      Moriarty (Norman McKinnell)

1932 Fox
      Sherlock Holmes
      Moriarty (Ernest Torrence)

1935 Fox
      Triumph of Sherlock Holmes
      Moriarty (Lyn Harding)

1940(?) Twentieth Century Fox
      Adventures of Sherlock Holmes
      Moriarty (George Zucco)

1942 Universal
      Sherlock Holmes and the Secret Weapon
      Moriarty (Lionel Atwill)

1945 Universal
      The Woman in Green
      Moriarity (Henry Daniell)

Sherlock Holmes in the theatre

1901 The Lyceum Theatre
      Sherlock Holmes
      Play by William Gillette
      Moriarty (W. L. Abingdon)

1905 The Duke of York's Theatre
      Sherlock Holmes
      Play by William Gillette
      Moriarty (George Sumner)

1953 Sadler's Wells Theatre
      The Great Detective
      Ballet by Margaret Dale
      Moriarty (Kenneth MacMillan)

1974 The Aldwych Theatre
      Moriarty (Philip Locke)

Sherlock Holmes in print

Moriarty first appeared in 1893 in the Sherlock Holmes stories published in *The Strand* Magazine.

The Memoirs of Sherlock Holmes

1894 George Newnes (London)

1907 Nelson's Library (London)

1920 George Newnes (London)

1924 Hodder and Stoughton (London), *The Memoirs* and *The Adventures of Sherlock Holmes* (with plates including portraits)

1930 John Murray (London), *The Memoirs* and *Adventures of Sherlock Holmes*

The Return of Sherlock Holmes

1905 George Newnes (London)

1907 Newnes sixpenny copyright novels (London)

1913 Newnes sixpenny copyright novels (London)

1925 Sir Isaac Pitman (Shorthand version) London

1960 John Murray (London)

Cain

From **The Bible**

'Adam knew Heva his wyfe; Who conceavynge, bare Cain, saying I have gotten a man of the Lorde. And she proceadynge furth brought furth hys brother Abel, and Abel was a keper of shepe. But Cain was a tyller of the grounde. And in processe of dayes it came to passe, that Caine brought of the frute of the grounde an oblacyon unto the Lorde. Abel also brought of the fyrstlynges of hys shepe, and of the fat thereof. And the Lorde had respecte unto Abel, and to hys oblacyon. But unto Cain and hys offrynge he had no respecte. For the which cause Cain was exceadyng wroth, and hys countenance abated. And the Lorde sayde unto Cain; Why art thou wrothe, and why is thy countenance abated? Yf thou do well shall there not be a promotion. And yf thou dost not well lyeth not thy sin in the dores? Unto thee also pertayneth the lust thereof, and thou shalt have dominion over it. And Cain spake unto Abel hys brother; Let us go furth.'
The Cranmer Byble 1540
(The first authorised English version)

'Cain said unto his brother Abel, "Let us go into the open country". While they were there, Cain attacked his brother Abel and murdered him. Then the Lord said to Cain, "Where is your brother Abel?" Cain answered, "I do not know. Am I my brother's keeper?" The Lord said, "What have you done? Hark! Your brother's blood that has been shed is crying out to me from the ground. Now you are accursed, and banished from the ground which has opened its mouth wide to receive your brother's blood, which you have shed. When you till the ground, it will no longer yield you its wealth. You shall be a vagrant and a wanderer on earth." Cain said to the Lord, "My punishment is heavier than I can bear; thou hast driven me today from the ground, and I must hide myself from thy presence. I shall be a vagrant and a wanderer on earth, and anyone who meets me can kill me." The Lord answered him. "No; if anyone kills Cain, Cain shall be avenged seven fold." So the Lord put a mark on Cain, in order that anyone meeting him should not kill him. Then Cain went out from the Lord's presence and settled in the land of Nod, to the east of Eden.

'Then Cain lay with his wife; and she conceived and bore Enoch. Cain was then building a city, which he named Enoch after his son.'
The New English Bible
(first published 1970)

Previous page: The 1966 screen version of
The Bible. Above: two much earlier
interpretations.

Two Hebrew Myths

When Cain and Abel were ready to marry, Adam
told Cain he must take Abel's twin sister, Quelimath
and that Abel must take Cain's sister, Lebhudha.
But Cain desired his own more beautiful sister.
Adam forbade this, warning Cain that he would be
guilty of incest. He ordered the brothers to each
make a sacrifice before his marriage. Cain's offering
was refused, and Satan persuaded him to kill Abel
for the sake of Lebhudha.

After Cain's banishment following the murder of
Abel, he had a son, Enoch. God allowed him to
rest from his wanderings and build a city, which he
named after his son. He founded six more cities—
Mauli, Leeth, Teze, Iesca, Celeth and Tabbath. His
wife Therec bore him three more sons Olad,
Lizaoh and Fosal, and two daughters, Citha and
Maac. Cain lived a corrupt life, and was a harsh
ruler. He put up boundaries around fields, and built
walled cities that he forced his people to live in. His
invention of weights and measures put an end to
man's simplicity.

The Bible on film

1966   Director Dino de Laurentis, Cain (Richard
       Harris)

Ballet

1968   *Cain and Abel*, choreography by Kenneth
       Macmillan at the Deutsches Oper, Berlin

The Bible on stage

The Wakefield and York Mystery Plays.
Religious cycles of plays performed in the open air
on Corpus Christi day—the first Thursday after
Trinity Sunday, in the middle of the fifteenth
century.

Each craft guild was given a scene from the Bible
to perform, and it is believed that the story of Cain
and Abel fell to the Company of Glovers in the York
cycle.

1961   *The Wakefield Mystery Play* revived at the
       Mermaid Theatre in London.

The Bible in print

(*A selected list*)

Biblion—scroll or paper ⎫ Greek
Biblia—writings   ⎭

8th Century   Portions of the Bible translated into
              Anglo Saxon
              The greater part of the Gospel of St.
              John translated by the Venerable Bede

1525   Unauthorised translation of the Bible
              into English, by William Tyndale.
              Copies brought into England were
              destroyed by the Bishops

1535   Archbishop Cranmer authorised the
              Coverdale translation of the Bible into
              English

1611   An English version authorised by King
              James I – The 'Authorised Version'

1881 – 5   The 'Revised Version'

1970   The New English Bible
              (The Bible in modern English idiom)

Godfrey Ablewhite

From **The Moonstone** By **Wilkie Collins**

'He stood over six feet high; he had a beautiful red and white colour; a smooth round face, shaved as bare as your hand; and a head of lovely long flaxen hair, falling negligently over the poll of his neck. But why do I try to give you this personal description of him? If you ever subscribed to a Ladies Charity in London, you know Mr Godfrey Ablewhite as well as I do. He was a barrister by profession; a ladies man by temperament; and a good Samaritan by choice. Female benevolence and female destitution could do nothing without him. Maternal societies for confining poor women; Magdalen societies for rescuing poor women; strong-minded societies for putting poor women into poor men's places, and leaving the men to shift for themselves; he was vice-president, manager, referee to them all. Wherever there was a table with a committee of ladies sitting round it in council, there was Mr Godfrey at the bottom of the board, keeping the temper of the committee, and leading the dear creatures along the thorny ways of business, hat in hand. I so suppose this was the most accomplished philanthropist (on a small independence) that England ever produced. As a speaker at charities the like of him for drawing your tears and your money was not easy to find. He was quite a public character. The last time I was in London, my mistress gave me two treats. She sent me to the theatre to see a dancing woman who was all the rage; and she sent me to Exeter Hall to hear Mr Godfrey. The lady did it, with a band of music. The gentleman did it, with a handkerchief and a glass of water. Crowds at the performance with the legs. Ditto at the performance with the tongue. And with all this the sweetest tempered person (I allude to Mr. Godfrey)—the simplest and pleasantest and easiest to please—you ever met with. He loved everybody. And everybody loved *him*. What chance had Mr Franklin—what chance had anybody of average reputation and capacities—against such a man as this?
Wilkie Collins

The Story

The Honourable Caroline Herncastle antagonised her family by marrying Mr Ablewhite, a rich but untitled banker. The marriage, although not blissful, was an adequate one, and they produced a large family. Their second son is Godfrey. He has become a barrister, a philanthropist and ladies' man. This is the public face of Ablewhite. His private face is in the suburbs where he keeps his mistress in a luxurious villa. He has been made joint trustee to the fortune of a young man on whose twenty-first birthday he is bound to hand over the sum of twenty thousand pounds. Ablewhite forges the signature of the joint trustee and draws out the twenty thousand pounds to pay for his expensive mistress. He must now find the means of replacing the twenty thousand pounds. He proposes to his cousin, Rachel Verinder, a potential heiress, and to a wealthy woman connected with his charity work. Both refuse him. Rachel Verinder inherits the Moonstone, a priceless diamond which, stolen from the Sultan of Seringapatam by John Herncastle, has remained in his family for fifty years. The diamond was followed to England by three Indians whose mission is to restore it to its rightful owners. Ablewhite steals the diamond and uses it as security for a loan of three thousand pounds, to be redeemed in one year's time. He receives a legacy of five thousand pounds which he uses to go to Amsterdam where he makes arrangements for the Moonstone to be cut up on its redemption. A year later he returns to England in disguise and reclaims the diamond. But he is followed by the Indians. The night before his return to Amsterdam with the Moonstone, they break into the bedroom of the public house where he is staying, and smother him with a pillow. They take the diamond and return it to India.

The Background

The Moonstone has been credited as the first English detective novel. But before it appeared on 4 January 1868 in Charles Dickens' periodical *All The Year Round*, an intriguing tale, *The Notting Hill Mystery*, kept readers of another magazine, *Once a Week*, enthralled from its first instalment in November 1862. The story is told in letters and reports sent to his employers by Ralph Henderson, investigator for a Life Assurance company. The case concerns the death of Madam R. after her husband, Baron R. has taken out large policies on her life. Not surprisingly Henderson suspects Baron R. of murder. He discovers him to be a German named Carl Schwartz, who possesses mesmeric powers. Unfortunately Henderson has no proof of the

Jameson Thomas as Ablewhite in the 1934 screen version *The Moonstone*.

Baron's guilt and the mystery remains unsolved.

The Notting Hill Mystery proved so popular that it was put into book form in 1865—three years before *The Moonstone*. The serialisation was published anonymously but the novel was credited to Charles Felix.

The plot of *The Notting Hill Mystery* is thought to have been taken from a court case of the time, a method which Wilkie Collins himself often employed, notably for *The Woman in White*.

The Moonstone on film

1911 Urban Production Company
1934 Pathe
Director Reg Barker
Ablewhite (Jameson Thomas)

The Moonstone in the theatre

1877 The Olympic Theatre (London)
play by Wilkie Collins from his novel

The Moonstone in print

(A selected list)

First serialised in the magazine 'conducted' by Charles Dickens, *All the Year Round* from 4 January 1868

1868	Tinsley Bros (London), 3 volumes
1871	Smith, Elder & Co (London)
1895	Chatto & Windus (London)
1925	Nelson's Classics (London)
1928	Oxford University Press (Oxford) Introduction by T. S. Eliot
1931	The Detective Story Club (for Collins, Sons & Co (London))
1944	J. M. Dent & Sons (London), E. P. Dutton (New York)
1951	The Folio Society, Lithographs by Edwin La Dell
1953	Collins (London and Glasgow), Introduction by G. D. H. and Margaret Cole
1955	Penguin (Harmondsworth)
1950	Longmans, Green & Co (London), adapted and simplified by E. M. Attwood
1959	Limited Editions Club, illustrated by Dignimont, Introduction by Vincent Stannett
1961	Blackie (London & Glasgow), illustrated by by Peter Edwards
1965	Harper & Row (New York and Evanston)
1967	Pan Books (London)
1969	Heron Books (London)
1963	Oxford University Press (Oxford)

Bill Sikes

From **Oliver Twist** By **Charles Dickens**

'A stoutly built fellow of about five and thirty, in a
black velveteen coat, very soiled drab breeches,
lace-up half boots, and grey cotton stockings, which
enclosed a very bulky pair of legs, with large
swelling calves—the kind of legs that, in such
costume, always look in an unfinished and incom-
plete state without a set of fetters to garnish them.
He had a brown hat on his head, and a dirty belcher
handkerchief around his neck; with the long, frayed
ends of which he smeared the beer from his face as
he spoke; disclosing, when he had done so, a broad
heavy countenance with a beard of three days'
growth; and two scowling eyes; one of which dis-
played various parti-coloured symptoms of having
been recently damaged by a blow.'
Charles Dickens

**Robert Newton as Sikes in the 1948 screen
version of *Oliver Twist*.**

The Story

A particularly brutal and hated criminal, Bill Sikes lives with his dog, Bullseye, and Nancy, a prostitute, in the back streets of London. Both Bill and Nancy belong to a gang run by Fagin, an evil but resourceful Jew, who keeps a number of boys that he trains in the art of pickpocketing. One of the boys, Oliver Twist, arouses the sympathy of Nancy. Her attempts to help him lead, unintentionally, to the uncovering of the gang. Seeking his revenge, Fagin tells Sikes that it is Nancy who has betrayed them, and in uncontrollable fury, Sikes batters Nancy to death. In terror he tries to escape from the law. Pursued in his imagination by the dead eyes of Nancy, he is finally trapped in the upstairs room of Fagin's house. As he tries to escape by means of a rope he once again sees the ghostly eyes. Paralysed with fear he slips and hangs himself. The dog attempts to jump on to his shoulders as he hangs there, loses its grip and falls to its death.

The Background

On 22 August 1836, Charles Dickens signed an agreement to edit and write serial stories for the periodical *Bently's Miscellany*. His first story was *Oliver Twist*. Dealing as it does with criminal life in the raw it met with a great deal of Victorian disapproval. In the third edition of the book Dickens wrote a preface explaining to his critics that his aim was to show the characters as they really were '. . . in all the squalid poverty of their lives . . . it appeared to me that to do this would be to attempt something that was greatly needed, and which would be a service to society. . . .'

Of Sikes, Dickens wrote: '. . . of one thing I am certain; that there are such men as Sikes, who, being closely followed through the same space of time, and through the same current of circumstances, would not give by one look or action of a moment, the faintest indication of a better nature. Whether every gentler human feeling is dead within such bosoms, or the proper chord to strike has rusted and is hard to find, I do not know; but the fact is so, I am sure. . . .'

A nineteenth-century drawing of Sikes by F. W. Pailthorpes.

Left: Bransby Williams as Sikes in about 1900.

Bill Sikes (*Oliver Twist*) on film

1909	Vitagraph
1910	Cosmopolitan (France)
1911	Cines (Italy)
1912	H. A. Spanuth Co (USA)
1912	Hepworth (UK). Sikes played by Harry Royston
1916	Paramount
1922	First National
1933	Monogram
1948	Cineguild. Sikes played by Robert Newton
1968	Romulus Films. Screen version of the musical *Oliver*; Sikes played by Oliver Reed.

Bill Sikes in the theatre

1838	The Surrey Theatre	Adapted by George Newman
1839	The Adelphi Theatre	Edward Stirling
1868	The Queen's Theatre	John Oxenford
1905	His Majesty's	J. Comyns Carr
1905	His Majesty's	J. Comyns Carr
1912	His Majesty's	J. Comyns Carr
1915	His Majesty's	J. Comyns Carr
1960	New Theatre (Musical 'Oliver')	Lionel Bart

Dickens himself gave public dramatised readings of his works. One of the most successful of these was Sikes' murder of Nancy. His reading of this scene was said to be frighteningly realistic and many were the occasions when ladies were carried from the audience in a dead faint.

Bill Sikes in print

Oliver Twist first appeared in print in the periodical *Bently's Miscellany*, which Dickens edited for a while, in February 1837.

1838	Richard Bently (London), illustrated by George Cruikshank
1839	Richard Bently (London), 3 volumes
1839	Lea and Blanchard (Philadelphia)
1841	Chapman and Hall (London), 3 volumes

The frontispiece to the Dick's (Penny) Play as performed at the Surrey Theatre in 1838.

Captain Hook

From **Peter and Wendy** By **James Barrie**

'In person he was cadaverous and blackavized, and his hair was dressed in long curls, which at a little distance looked like black candles, and gave a singularly threatening expression to his handsome countenance. His eyes were of the blue of the for-get-me-not, and of a profound melancholy, save when he was plunging his hook into you, at which time two red spots appeared in them and lit them up horribly. In manner, something of the grand signeur still clung to him, so that he even ripped you up with an air, and I have been told that he was a raconteur of repute. He was never more sinister than when he was most polite, which is probably the truest test of breeding; and the elegance of his diction, even when he was swearing, no less the distinction of his demeanour, showed him one of a different caste from his crew. A man of indomitable courage it was said that the only thing he shied at was the sight of his own blood, which was thick and of an unusual colour. In dress he somewhat aped the attire associated with the name of Charles II, having heard it said in some earlier period of his career that he bore a strange resemblance to the ill-fated Stuarts; and in his mouth he had a holder of his own contrivance which enabled him to smoke two cigars at once. But undoubtedly the grimmest part of him was his iron claw.'

James Barrie

Right: Captain Hook in the 1952 Walt Disney Production of *Peter Pan*.

The Story

In the Neverland, James Hook, late of Eton and Balliol College, Oxford, blackhearted Captain of the pirate ship 'The Jolly Roger', and his crew of pirates, hunt Peter Pan and his band of lost boys. Hook's right arm (now replaced by an iron hook) was cut off by Peter and thrown to a passing crocodile which so liked the taste of it that it follows Hook everywhere hoping for a second helping. Hook and his men capture the lost boys, along with Wendy, John and Michael Darling who have been brought to the Neverland as Peter's guests. They are taken aboard 'The Jolly Roger' and held prisoner. But Peter comes to their rescue and he and Hook fight a duel to the death which ends when Peter corners Hook and kicks him over the side of the ship—straight into the open jaws of the waiting crocodile.

The Background

On 7 July 1927, James Barrie delivered a speech to the 'First Hundred' at Eton to prove that James Hook was 'a good Etonian, but not a great one'. Barrie told of Hook's early days at Eton and Balliol. Of his athletic achievement (12th man in the college 100 yards at Balliol), his Eton colours (his Aunt Emily had three of his caps hanging over her mantelpiece—he had them especially made at a little place in the city), his yellow blood which 'saved him many lammings from the head of the house, who though keeper of the fives, fainted at first sight of it'. Barrie told of Hook's return to Eton after he was deceased, when a certain Mr Jasparin suddenly came upon him sitting on a wall and saw him deny, for the honour of the school, his old Etonian status, to a policeman, who challenged his right to be thus seated. How he appeared again in the said Mr Jasparin's room, silent and melancholy. During his stay he must have managed to strike his own name from the Etonian records—certainly they are no longer there.

'To obliterate the memory of himself from the tabernacle he had fouled was all this erring son of Eton could do for his beloved. In that one moment of time was he not a good Etonian?'

Peter Pan on film

1924 Paramount: Directed by Herbert Brenon
Captain Hook (Ernest Torrence)

1952 Walt Disney Productions
(full length feature cartoon)

Peter Pan in the theatre

Peter Pan opened at the Duke of York's Theatre in 1904 with Nina Bouticault as Peter and Gerald du Maurier as Captain Hook.
Notable Captain Hooks: Alastair Sim, Eric Porter, Ron Moody, Dave Allen, Michael Dennison, Donald Sinden

"THIS MAN IS MINE"

A drawing by F. D. Bedford from the 1911 edition of *Peter Pan*.

Peter Pan in print

(A selected list)

Mr Barrie's speech, delivered to the 'First Hundred' at Eton on 7 July 1927, was recorded in full in *The Times* on 8 July 1927

1907   *Peter Pan keepsake* (retold from Mr Barrie's fantasy). Chatto & Windus (London), edited by Daniel O'Connor, Foreword by W. T. Stead

1911   Hodder & Stoughton (London), illustrated by F. D. Bedford and Mabel Lucie Atwell

1915   Hodder & Stoughton (London), illustrated by F. D. Bedford

1921   Hodder & Stoughton (London), illustrated by Mabel Lucie Atwell

1925   Retold by May Byron for boys and girls. Hodder & Stoughton (London), illustrated by Mabel Lucie Atwell

1931   Hodder & Stoughton (London), decorated by G. M. Hudson

1934   Oxford University Press (Oxford)

1938   *The Nursery Peter Pan and Wendy* (retold by Kathleen Byron). Hodder & Stoughton (London), illustrated by Kathleen Atkins

1939   Hodder & Stoughton (London), illustrated by Edmund Blampied

1942   Hodder & Stoughton (London), illustrated by John Morton Sale

1951   Hodder & Stoughton (London), illustrated by Nora S. Unwin

1952   Walt Disney's Peter Pan

1955   Retold by Arthur Groom. Binn Bros (London), with five pop-up pictures

1957   Juvenile Production of James Barrie's *Peter Pan & Wendy*. Samuel French (New York & London)

1962   *The Story of the Play* by Eleanor Graham and Edward Ardizzone. Puffin (Harmondsworth)

1964   *Peter Pan* (a fantasy in five acts). Samuel French (New York & London)

1964   Hodder & Stoughton (London) (Acting Edition)

Chauvelin

From **The Scarlet Pimpernel** By **Baroness Orczy**

'. . . the man who had spoken was sitting by the table, with elbows resting thereon. His long, claw-like fingers were interlocked and made a support for his chin. He was a small spare man who would have appeared insignificant but for his pale, sunken eyes, which now and then flashed with a cold, glittering light like those of a cat on the prowl in the night. He was dressed in sober black and wore his dark hair tied at the nape of the neck with a black bow. . . .

'He paused for a moment, his pale eyes fixed on the woman as a snake fixes its eyes on the prey it covets . . . picked up a long quill, held it between two claw-like fingers and toyed with it, tap-tapping it against the table. . . .'

Baroness Orczy

Horace Hodges as Chauvelin in the 1905 production of the play.

The Story

During the French Revolution the French Republican government sends Chauvelin, their fox-like chief of police, to England as their official representative, with instructions to investigate the elusive English champions of the aristocratic victims of the Revolution, known as the League of the Scarlet Pimpernel. Believed popularly to be led by an English nobleman known only as 'The Scarlet Pimpernel'. In England he contacts an old acquaintance, Marguerite St. Just, once an actress famous in France for her glittering salons and now married to the English baronet, Sir Percy Blakeney. Under threat of her brother Armand's imprisonment for anti-revolutionary activities, she promises to help Chauvelin uncover the identity of the Pimpernel. To Marguerite's horror she discovers, too late, the identity she is helping to expose is none other than her own husband. With this knowledge Chauvelin starts on the long series of cat and mouse games that he hopes will lead eventually to the capture of Sir Percy Blakeney and his companions—The League of the Scarlet Pimpernel.

The Background

Baroness Orczy's first attempts to sell *The Scarlet Pimpernel* were a miserable failure. The first offer from a publisher was the grand sum of £30 for all of the rights. It was not until she hit upon the idea of selling a play based on the story that the publishers began to show more interest. In 1903 the Terry management accepted the play. The publisher's offer of £30 for the book was on condition that the play was produced simultaneously. But Baroness Orczy turned the offer down. Once again the manuscript was in the post to another publisher,

Greening & Co. The news that came back was good. They would accept the book, but as before, the condition was publication of the book on the production of the play. This time, however, the financial terms were more realistic, and Baroness Orczy accepted. The book was finally published in 1905 and became a best seller.

The 'Scarlet Pimpernel' adventures brought fame on a grand scale to Baroness Orczy. She was something of a celebrity in her own right. But in the public's acceptance of the book Sir Percy did not always have it his own way. At a party Baroness Orczy was approached by a 'sandwich chewing lady' who gushed through a spray of crumbs: 'I loved your *lovely* book! What a marvellous hero Chauvelin is! . . .'

The Scarlet Pimpernel on film

Silent

1928   *The Triumph of the Scarlet Pimpernel*
        (Re-entitled *The Scarlet Daredevil* in America)
        Produced by Herbert Wilcox

Sound

1935   London Film/United Artists
        The Triumph of the Scarlet Pimpernel
        Leslie Howard as Blakeney
        Raymond Massey as Chauvelin
        Produced by Alexander Korda

1937   London Films/United Artists
        The Return of the Scarlet Pimpernel
        Barry K. Barnes as Blakeney
        Francis Lister as Chauvelin
        Produced by Alexander Korda

1959   Warner Bros. Cartoon
        The Scarlet Pimpernickel
        Starring Duffy Duck

Raymond Massey as Chauvelin in the 1935 screen version.

The Scarlet Pimpernel in the theatre

1905   The New Theatre
play by Baroness Orczy and
Montague Barstow
Chauvelin (Horace Hodges)
(originally produced at the Theatre Royal,
Nottingham (1903)

The Scarlet Pimpernel in print

(A selected list)

1905   *The Scarlet Pimpernel.* Greening & Co
(London)
1906   *I Will Repay.* Greening & Co (London)
1908   *The Elusive Pimpernel.* Hutchinson & Co
(London)

1913   *Eldorado.* Hodder & Stoughton (London)
1917   *Lord Tony's Wife.* Hodder & Stoughton
(London)
1919   *League of the Scarlet Pimpernel.* Cassell & Co
(London)
1922   *Triumph of the Scarlet Pimpernel.* Hodder &
Stoughton (London)
1927   *Sir Percy Hits Back.* Hodder & Stoughton
(London)
1929   *Adventures of the Scarlet Pimpernel.*
Hutchinson & Co (London)
1936   *Sir Percy Leads the Band.* Hodder &
Stoughton (London)
1940   *Mam'zelle Guillotine.* Hodder & Stoughton
(London)

Omnibus Editions

1930   *Scarlet Pimpernel Omnibus.* Hodder &
Stoughton (London)
(*Scarlet Pimpernel, I Will Repay, Eldorado,
Sir Percy Hits Back*)
Gallant Pimpernel Omnibus

**Horace Hodges in another still from the 1905
production.**

Count Dracula

From **Dracula** By **Bram Stoker**

Below: A fifteenth-century woodcut of
Vlad V Dracula.

'His face was a strong—a very strong—aqualine,
with high bridge of the nose and peculiarly arched
nostrils; with lofty domed forehead, and hair growing scantily round the temples, but profusely else-
where. His eyebrows were very massive, almost
meeting over the nose, and with bushy hair that
seemed to curl in its own profusion. The mouth, so
far as I could see it under the heavy moustache was
fixed and rather cruel looking, with peculiarly sharp,
white teeth; these protruded over the lips, whose
remarkable ruddiness showed astonishing vitality in
a man of his years. For the rest, his ears were pale
and at the tops extremely pointed; the chin was
broad and strong, and the cheeks firm though thin.
The general effect was one of extraordinary pallor.
   Hitherto I had noticed the back of his hands as
they lay on his knees in the firelight, and they had
seemed rather white and fine; but seeing them now
close to me, I could not but notice that they were
rather coarse-broad, with squat fingers. Strange to
say there were hairs in the centre of the palm. The
nails were long and fine and cut to a sharp point.
As the Count leaned over me and his hands touched
me, I could not repress a shudder. It may have
been that his breath was rank, but a horrible feeling
of nausea came over me, which, do what I would,
I could not conceal.'
Bram Stoker

35

Bela Lugosi as Dracula in the 1931 screen version.

The Story

Dracula, king of the vampires, or the undead, is entombed in Castle Dracula, in Transylvania. Between the hours of sunset and sunrise he leaves the grave and seeks female victims whose blood will sustain him until the next sunset. He sinks his long, fang-like teeth into their necks and sucks their life blood. The victims die and become she vampires. Dracula transports himself to England. But here he is discovered by the friends of one of his victims. Led by the Dutch Professor Abraham Van Helsing, they pursue him back to Transylvania where they trap and finally destroy him by driving a stake through his heart and cutting off his head.

Dracul is the Rumanian name for Devil. After long discussions on the supernatural with Hall Caine and Henry Irving, mixed with old memories of the story of a female vampire, Carmilla, but according to himself, more on account of a too generous helping of dressed crab for supper, Bram (Abraham) Stoker had a dream which he remembered and wrote down. It became the story of Dracula. Stoker based his character on the real life Vlad V Dracula a voivode, or prince, who ruled the Walachian principality of Muntenia, on the Transylvanian border, from 1456 to 1462 and again from 1475 to 1476. Infamous for his great cruelty, his favourite method of execution earned him the nickname 'The Impaler'. But in spite of this he is said to have been a just ruler who freed his country from the invading Turks. Antonio Bonfini, the chronicler of King Matthias Corvinus of Hungary, wrote: 'It is said that this Dracula is an unbelievably cruel but *just* man.'

Dracula on film

1922 Prana Films
Nosferatu (Max Schrek)

1931 Universal
Dracula (Bela Lugosi)

1936 Universal
Dracula's Daughter (Bela Lugosi)

1943 Universal
Son of Dracula (Lon Chaney Jnr)

1944 Universal
House of Frankenstein (John Carradine)

1945 Universal
House of Dracula (John Carradine)

1948 Universal
Abbott and Costello meet Frankenstein (Bela Lugosi)

1957 American/International
Blood of Dracula

1958 Hammer
Horror of Dracula (In Britain *Dracula*) (Christopher Lee)

1960 Hammer
The Brides of Dracula

1965 Hammer
Dracula, Prince of Darkness

1968 Hammer
Dracula has risen from the grave

1969 A & E Film Corporation
Blood of Dracula's Castle (John Carradine)

1969 Hammer/Warner/Seven Arts
Taste the Blood of Dracula (Christopher Lee)

1970 Hammer/EMI
Scars of Dracula (Christopher Lee)

1970 Fenix Films (Madrid)
Dracula (Christopher Lee)
(Distributed by Hemdale in 1974)

1973 Dan Curtis Production made for television
(Jack Palance)
(Distributed by EMI)

Dracula in the theatre

1897 Royal Lyceum Theatre
Dramatisation by Bram Stoker
(staged for one night only to establish copyright)
Dracula played by Mr Jones

1925 Wimbledon Theatre
Dramatised by Hamilton Deane
Dracula played by Raymond Huntley

1927 The Little Theatre
Dramatisation by Hamilton Deane
Dracula played by Raymond Huntley

1927 The Duke of York's Theatre
Dramatisation by Hamilton Deane
Dracula played by Raymond Huntley

1927 The Prince of Wales Theatre
Dramatisation by Hamilton Deane
Dracula played by Raymond Huntley

1927 The Schubert Theatre, New Haven, Connecticut
Dramatisation by H. Deane & John Balderston
Dracula played by Bela Lugosi

A cartoon by E. S. Hughes of the 1927 dramatisation of *Dracula* by Hamilton Deane at The Little Theatre. Dracula was played by Raymond Huntley.

1927 The Garrick Theatre
Dramatisation by Hamilton Deane
Dracula played by Raymond Huntley

1939 The Winter Garden Theatre

1939 The Lyceum Theatre

Dracula in print

(*A selected list*)

1897 A. Constable and Co (Westminster)

1897 Doubleday and MacClure (New York)

1909 Doubleday, Page and Co (New York)

1912 William Rider and Son (London)

1913 Garden City, Doubleday, Page and Co (New York)

1916 William Rider and Sons (London)

1917 Garden City, Doubleday, Page and Co (New York)

1919 William Rider and Sons (London)

1928 Grossett and Dunlap (New York)

1932 The Modern Library (New York)

1947 Pocket Book (New York)

1957 Permabook (New York)

1959 Garden City (New York)

1959 Doubleday (Toronto)

1962 Arrow Books (London)

1966 Jarrolds (London)

1974 Sphere Books (London)

'Dracula's Guest' was part of the original novel as written by Bram Stoker. When Dracula was published it was excluded as it was thought that it would make the book too long. It was printed as a short story after Stoker's death

1914 *Dracula's Guest, and other weird stories*
George Routledge & Sons (London)

1927 *Dracula's Guest*
(Souvenir edition for presentation to the audience at the Prince of Wales Theatre on the occasion of the 250th London performance of the play 'Dracula' on 14 September)

1966 *Dracula's Guest.* Hutchinson

1966 *Dracula's Guest.* Jarrolds (London)

1966 *Dracula's Guest.* Arrow Books (London)

Dom Claude Frollo

From **The Hunchback of Notre Dame** By **Victor Hugo**

'Among the thousand faces tinged by the scarlet light, there was one which seemed to be more than all the rest absorbed in the contemplation of the dancer. It was the face of a man, austere, calm and sombre. This man, whose costume was hidden by the crowd that surrounded him, seemed to be not more than thirty five years of age; yet he was bald, having only a few thin tufts of hair about his temples, which were already grey; his broad and high forehead was beginning to be furrowed with wrinkles; but in his deep-set eyes there shone an extraordinary youth, an intense animation, a depth of passion. . . .

'. . . from time to time a smile and a sigh met each other on his lips; but the smile was more sad than the sigh.'
Victor Hugo

The Story

Claude Frollo, a grave and studious boy, born into a wealthy family, had been trained by his parents for the church. In 1466 he was orphaned by the plague and dedicated his life to the church and the raising of his baby brother, Jehan. While a chaplain at Notre Dame he rescues a foundling baby, a deformed hunchback whom he calls Quasimodo. Quasimodo is devoted to Frollo who makes him the bellringer of Notre Dame.

Years pass and Frollo, now grown austere and morose, has become the Archdeacon of Jossa. He sees the gipsy girl Esmeralda dancing in the street and falls in love with her. With the help of Quasimodo he abducts her. She is rescued by Captain Phoebus de Chateaupeurs of the Night Guard. Frollo escapes, but Quasimodo is pilloried. He is pitied by Esmeralda who gives him water.

Frollo, hearing from his brother that Esmeralda has fallen in love with Captain Phoebus and has planned to meet him, is incredulous and full of jealous rage. For a fee, and to prove the truth of the rendezvous, the Captain allows Frollo to hide in the room where he is to meet Esmeralda. As Phoebus and Esmeralda are about to make love Frollo bursts from his hiding place, stabs Phoebus and runs away.

Esmeralda is arrested and, watched by Frollo in disguise, confesses under torture to sorcery and the murder of Phoebus. She is sentenced to death but is rescued at the eleventh hour by Quasimodo who carries her to sanctuary in the cathedral. Frollo hears that Phoebus is alive, and in his jealousy arranges for Esmeralda to leave Paris. But when Esmeralda realises who is helping her to escape she runs away from him. She is caught and hanged, Quasimodo, realising that Frollo is to blame for her death, throws him from the roof of the cathedral, and watches him crash to his death.

The Background

In 1828 Victor Hugo agreed to write a romance for the publisher Gosselin, set in the Paris of the Middle Ages and featuring the cathedral of Notre Dame. But he devoted his time to other books. In July 1830 Gosselin threatened Hugo with legal proceedings for breaking contract. Hugo was therefore spurred on to write his masterpiece. The book was published on 17 March 1831 when the newspapers were mainly concerned with the restoration of King Louis Philippe to the throne. *The Hunchback of Notre Dame* was therefore not fully acknowledged or appreciated until a few years later.

The Hunchback of Notre Dame on film

1923 Frollo (Nigel de Brulier)
1939 Frollo (Cedric Hardwick)
1956 Frollo (Alain)

The Hunchback of Notre Dame in the theatre

1834 Sadler's Wells Theatre
Play by C. Z. Barnett

1834 Adelphi Theatre
Esmeralda or *The Deformed Man of Notre Dame*, a musical drama by Edward Fitzball.

1836 Covent Garden Theatre
Quasimodo an opera by Edward Fitzball.

1850 Adelphi Theatre
Esmeralda a Burlesque by A. R. Simms.

1870 Grecian Theatre
The man with the hump or *The Bellringer of Notre Dame*, A Burlesque by Henry Spry

1871 East London Theatre
The Bellringer or the Hunchback's Love by S. W. H. Abel.

1879 Gaiety Theatre
Esmeralda.

Alain as Dom Claude Frollo in the 1956 screen version.

1883	Drury Lane Theatre *Esmeralda.* A Lyric Drama by T. Marzials and A. Ramdegger
1892	Surrey Theatre *Midnight* or *the Bell of Notre Dame* by A. Shirley.

Ballet

1844	Her Majesty's Theatre *Esmeralda*, music by Pugne, Choreography by Perrot (still in the repertoire in Russia)
1954	Festival Hall (Festival Ballet) *Esmeralda* music by Pugne, choreography by Beriozoff

Hunchback of Notre Dame in print

1831	Gosselin, vignettes by Tony Johannot
1833	Richard Bentley (London), translated with sketches of the life and writings of the author by Frederick Shobert
1844	Paris édition illustrée d'apres les dessins de M. M. E. de Beaumont, L. Boulanger, Daubigny, T. Johannot

1853	J. Hetzel (Paris), illustrated by Gerard Sequin.
1862	—(New York), translated by H. C. Williams
1876	Hachette et Cie (Paris)
1885	Geo. Routledge and Sons (London), illustrated
1891	Sampson Low and Co, illustrated by Bieler, Rossi and Myrback, Translated by A. L. Alger
1902	Ginn & Co (Boston, Mass), Introduction by J. R. Wightman
1908	Nelson's Classics (London)
1928	G. G. Harrap & Co (London), illustrated by Roland Wheelwright
1930	The Limited Editions Club (London), 2 volumes, Translated by Jessie Haynes, illustrated by Frans Masereel
1953	Collins (London & Glasgow), translated by J. Carroll Beckwith, introduced by M. L. M. Young
1956	Bantam Books (New York), Translated by Lowell Blair

Cedric Hardwick as Dom Claude Frollo in the 1939 screen version.

Cruella De Vil

From **The Hundred and One Dalmatians** By **Dodie Smith**

'At that moment, the peace was shattered by an extremely strident motor horn. A large car was coming towards them. It drew up at a big house just ahead of them and a tall woman came out on to the front door steps. She was wearing a tight fitting satin dress, several ropes of rubies, and an absolutely simple white mink cloak, which reached to the high heels of her ruby-red shoes. She had a dark skin, black eyes with a tinge of red in them, and a very pointed nose. Her hair was parted severely down the middle and one half of it was black and the other white—rather unusual. . . .'
Dodie Smith

The Story

Cruella De Vil (the girl with two-coloured hair, one side white, one side black) was expelled from school for drinking ink. Even at that age she was as feared and disliked as her evil and mysterious ancestors of Hell Hall, in Suffolk. Because of her passionate craving for furs, she married a furrier (although she kept her own name as she was the last of the De Vils). She willingly resorts to any form of cruelty to obtain animal skins. She likes roaring fires and takes pepper with all her food. She and her husband live near Regent's Park and let Hell Hall to two toughs,

Cruella de Vil in the 1960 Walt Disney version.

41

the Badduns, who act as keepers to a large number of stolen dalmatian puppies. The puppies are hidden at Hell Hall until they are bigger and worth killing for their skins. Cruella steals more dalmatians from an old school acquaintance. But the father and mother of the pups discover where they are hidden by way of the bush telegraph (known as the Twilight Barking) and set off to the rescue. With the help of the other dogs on the 'Twilight Barking' network all of Cruella's prisoners are rescued, and her entire stock of furs destroyed. Her black hair turns white, and her white hair turns green with shock. She and her husband hurriedly leave the country to start a plastic mackintosh business abroad.

The Background

Hell Hall, ancestral home of the De Vils, was once Hill Hall, owned by a farmer named Hill. He got into debt and sold it to one of Cruella's ancestors. His intention was to build a fantastic house—a mixture of castle and cathedral. He began by erecting a surrounding wall. Once it was finished strange

rumours began to spread of screams and wild laughter coming from the Hall and of De Vil being the possessor of a long tail. The place from then onwards was called Hell Hall, and De Vil became devil. One night some villagers attacked the Hall intending to burn it down, but a sudden thunderstorm put out their torches, the gates burst open and De Vil rode through in a coach and four surrounded by lightning which appeared to come, not from the skies, but from him. The villagers fled screaming. When Cruella took over Hell Hall she had it painted black outside and red inside.

Cruella De Vil on film

1960   Walt Disney Productions

Cruella De Vil in print

(*A selected list*)

1956   *The Hundred and One Dalmatians*. Heinemann (London), illustrated by Janet & Anne Graham Johnstone

1961   Puffin, Harmondsworth, with the original illustrations

Cruella de Vil by Janet and Anne Graham Johnstone.

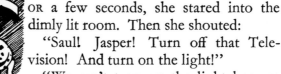

OR a few seconds, she stared into the dimly lit room. Then she shouted: "Saul! Jasper! Turn off that Television! And turn on the light!"

"We can't turn on the light because we've no electric bulbs left," said Saul Baddun. "When the Telly finishes, we go to bed."

Dorian Gray

From The Picture of Dorian Gray by Oscar Wilde

'Lord Henry looked at him. Yes, he was certainly wonderfully handsome, with his finely curved scarlet lips, his frank blue eyes, his crisp gold hair. There was something in his face that made one trust him at once. All the candour of youth was there, as well as youth's passionate purity. One felt that he had kept himself unspotted from the world.'
Oscar Wilde

The Story

Lord Kelso, angry at his daughter's bad match with a penniless soldier causes his son-in-law to fight a duel in which he is killed. A year later his daughter also dies leaving an only child, Dorian Gray.

Dorian inherits his grandfather's wealth and his mother's beauty. A young artist, Basil Hallward, obsessed by Dorian, paints his portrait.

The portrait is seen by the suave and degenerate Lord Henry Wooton. Fascinated by it, he asks to meet Dorian, who immediately falls under his corrupting influence, and begins to live a life of decadent self indulgence. In horrified fascination he discovers that while his own beauty remains un-touched his portrait bears the brunt of his sins and excesses, becoming lined and raddled. He hides the portrait.

After many years, Dorian, his beauty still intact, is beginning to hate the futility of his life. He shows Hallward what has become of his portrait, then murders him in a fit of rage, seeing him as the original cause of his degeneracy. His crime is never discovered, but later he tries to destroy the picture with a knife, and is found—a loathsome, withered

Henry Keen's interpretation of Dorian Gray in the 1925 edition.

creature, lying stabbed to death beneath the portrait of a beautiful young man.

The Background

In 1890, at a time of his life when he was even more penniless than usual, Wilde received a commission from *Lippincotts Monthly* for a serialised novel. He produced *The Picture of Dorian Gray*, and at once became the centre of a public outcry. The story was branded as corrupt and his already shaky reputation suffered a severe and lasting blow, during his famous trial in 1895 against The Marquis of Queensberry. Wilde had brought a libel action against the Marquis, the father of his friend, Lord Alfred Douglas, which turned upon him and resulted in his own conviction for homosexual practice, and a subsequent prison sentence of two years.

At the trial the homosexual element in *The Picture of Dorian Gray* was used against him. The moral of the tale, that Dorian Gray's sins had 'found him out' does not seem to have been taken into account.

The Picture of Dorian Gray on film

Silent

1913　Ideal Films

Sound

1923　Stoll
1945　MGM
　　　Dorian Gray (Hurd Hatfield)
　　　(Film won 1945 Academy Award for photography)
1973　ABC/Television Production
　　　Dorian Gray (Shane Briant)

The Picture of Dorian Gray in the theatre

1947　The 'Q' Theatre
　　　Adapted by Constance Cox
　　　Dorian Gray (Vernon Greene)

The Picture of Dorian Gray in print

(*A selected list*)

First serialised in Lippincott's Monthly magazine June 1890

1891　Ward, Lock & Co. (London)
1904　Charterhouse Press (New York)
1908　Charles Canington (Paris, Edinburgh)
　　　Preface by Robert Press
1925　John Lane (London), Dodd Mead & Co (New York), illustrated by Henry Keen
1930　Horace Liveright (New York), illustrated by Majeska
1949　Penguin (Harmondsworth)
1960　Brown, Watson

Hurd Hatfield as Dorian Gray and Lowell Gilmore as
the artist in two stills from the 1945 screen version.

Edward Hyde

From **The Strange Case of Dr Jekyll and Mr Hyde** By **Robert Louis Stevenson**

'Mr Hyde was pale and dwarfish, he gave the impression of deformity without any nameable malformation, he had a displeasing smile, he had borne himself to the lawyer with a sort of murderous mixture of timidity and boldness, and he spoke with a husky, whispering and somewhat broken voice . . . he is not easy to describe. There is something wrong with his appearance; something downright detestable. I never saw a man I so disliked, and yet I scarce know why. He must be deformed somewhere he gives a strong feeling of deformity, although I couldn't specify the point. He's an extraordinary looking man, and yet I really can name nothing out of the way. No sir, I can make no hand of it; I can't describe him. And it's not want of memory; for I declare I can see him this moment. . . .'
Robert Louis Stevenson

The Story

The eminent and respected Dr Henry Jekyll is fascinated by his own tendencies towards a dual personality. His experiments lead to the discovery of a potion that will change him into his alter ego— a man he calls Edward Hyde. Hyde is the embodiment of all that is evil in Jekyll. Jekyll is now able to lead his normal life during the day and revert to the debaucheries of Mr Hyde at night without detection. But Hyde slowly begins to dominate Jekyll. He commits a brutal murder and is now hunted by the police. Just before he is discovered, and realising that Hyde is finally taking over, Jekyll swallows poison—killing himself and Edward Hyde.

The Background

The *Strange Case of Dr Jekyll and Mr Hyde* was written by Stevenson during one of his frequent bouts of ill-health. The idea was conceived in a terrifying dream from which he was awakened, shouting, by his wife. He sat up in his sick bed and finished his tale in three days. His wife thought it not good enough so he rewrote it. In 1886 Longmans published the book in a shilling edition. It was an immediate best seller. Stevenson, always interested in the potential duality of man, had already explored the subject in his play *Deacon Brodie* (The Double Life) written in 1879.

Two stills of H. B. Irving as Hyde in the 1910 stage production of *Jekyll and Hyde* at the Queens Theatre.

Edward Hyde on film

1908   Selig
Dr. Jekyll and Mr. Hyde

1910   Nordisk
Den Skaebnesvangre Opfindelse (Danish)
(Alwin Neuss)
(US *Dr. Jekyll and Mr Hyde*)

1912   Tannhauser
Dr Jekyll and Mr Hyde (James Cruze)

1913   Imperial
Dr Jekyll and Mr Hyde. (King Baggott)

1913   Kinemacolor
Dr Jekyll and Mr Hyde.

1920   Famous Players
Dr Jekyll and Mr Hyde (John Barrymore)

1920   Pioneer
Dr Jekyll and Mr Hyde (Sheldon Lewis)

1931   Paramount
Dr Jekyll and Mr Hyde (Fredric March)

1941   MGM
Dr Jekyll and Mr Hyde (Spencer Tracy)

1951   Columbia
Son of Dr Jekyll

1951   Sono
Il Dotor Jekyll

1953   Universal
Abbott and Costello meet Dr Jekyll and Mr Hyde (Boris Karloff)

1957   Allied Artists
Daughter of Dr Jekyll

1960   M.G.
Il Mio Amico Jekyll (Ugo Tognazzi)

1960   Hammer
The Two Faces of Dr Jekyll (Paul Massie)

1970   Amicus
Mr Hyde (Christopher Lee)

**Fredric March as Hyde in the 1931
screen version**

Edward Hyde in the theatre

1888   The Lyceum Theatre
        Play by T. R. Sullivan.
        Hyde (Richard Mansfield)

1910   The Queen's Theatre
        Play by J. Comyns Carr.
        Hyde (H. B. Irving)

1927   The Royal, Bath
        Play by Lena Ashwell and Roger Pocock
        Hyde (Wilfred Fletcher)

1927   The Century Theatre
        Play by Lena Ashwell and R. Pocock
        Hyde (Wilfred Fletcher)

Boris Karloff as Hyde in the 1953 screen adaptation: Abbott and Costello meet Dr Jekyll and Mr Hyde.

An illustration from the 1929 edition of the book.

Edward Hyde in print

(*A selected list*)

1886   Longmans and Co. (London)

1886   Longmans, Green and Co. (London)

1893   Longmans and Co. (London)

1925   Sir I. Pitman and Sons (London) (Printed in
        the Advanced Stage of Pitmans shorthand)

1929   W. Collins and Co. (London and Glasgow)

1929   Longmans and Co. (London), Wesleyan
        Methodist Book Depot, Cape Coast (edited
        and simplified by C. Kingsley Williams)

1930   John Lane (London) illustrated by S. G.
        Hulme Beaman

1946   Robert Grant and Son, Edinburgh, illustrated
        by Helen A. Martin

1948   Folio Society (London), illustrated by Mervyn
        Peake

1966   Thomas Nelson & Co (London)
        The Strange Case of Dr Jekyll and Mr Hyde
        can also be found in the collected works of
        Robert Louis Stevenson and many editions
        of shorter collected works.

Goldfinger

From **Goldfinger** By **Ian Fleming**

'When Goldfinger had stood up, the first thing that struck Bond was that everything was out of proportion. Goldfinger was short, not more than five feet tall, and on top of the thick body and blunt peasant legs, was set almost directly into the shoulders, a huge, and it seemed, exactly round head. It was as if Goldfinger had been put together with bits of other people's bodies. Nothing seemed to belong. Perhaps, Bond thought, it was to conceal his ugliness that Goldfinger made such a fetish of sunburn. Without the red brown camouflage the pale body would be grotesque. The face, under the cliff of crew-cut carroty hair, was startling, without being as ugly as the body. It was moon-shaped without being moon-like. The forehead was fine and high and the thin sandy brows were level above the large light blue eyes fringed with pale lashes. The nose was fleshily aquiline between high cheek bones and cheeks that were more muscular than fat. The mouth was thin and dead straight, but beautifully drawn. The chin and jaws were firm and glinted with health. To sum up, thought Bond, it was the face of a thinker, perhaps a scientist, who was ruthless, sensual, stoical and tough. An odd combination. . . .'
Ian Fleming

The Story

In 1937, at the age of 20, Auric Goldfinger arrives in England, a refugee from Riga. He starts making money buying and selling old jewellery and gold. In 1954 he is suspected of gold smuggling. A surreptitious, five-year investigation by the Bank of England shows him to be the richest man in Britain, with £20 million worth of gold, mostly English, melted down by him and kept in various parts of the world.

Secret Service agent 007, James Bond, is assigned to track down Goldfinger and bring the gold back to England. After tailing him through Europe, Bond is captured by him and forced to participate in an audacious and hitherto undreamed of crime—to rob Fort Knox of $15 billion worth of gold bullion! Bond manages to send word to the Secret Service and the raid is stopped in mid action. Goldfinger escapes and re-captures Bond, but is killed by him in a final and desperate struggle.

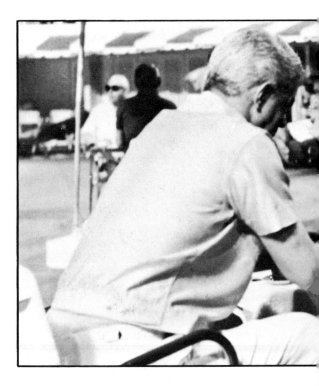

Background

In 1956 Ian Fleming was staying at a health clinic, Enton Hall, in Godalming, Surrey. It was here, whilst in the steam bath, that Fleming met Guy Welby, a goldsmith. During his stay at the clinic Fleming enthusiastically discussed gold with Welby. He found out how gold was tested, how it was stored, and how it was smuggled. In the summer of 1957, Goldfinger began to take shape in his mind. As well as Guy Welby he turned to his old friend Rickatson-Hall, at the Bank of England, for advice. His interest in gold and his passion for golf, feature prominently in the first half of the book. *Goldfinger* was, therefore, one of the easiest books for Fleming to write. He died in 1962, during the filming of *Goldfinger*.

Goldfinger on film

1964   Eon Films (Distributed by United Artists)

Goldfinger in print

1959   Jonathan Cape Ltd (London)
1961   Pan Books (London)
Goldfinger was also serialised in strip-cartoon form in the London *Daily Express*.

Left and above: two stills from the 1964 screen version with Gert Frobe as Goldfinger.

The *Daily Express* strip-cartoon by John McLusky.

James Bond
BY IAN FLEMING
DRAWING BY JOHN McLUSKY

BOND STRAINED AGAINST THE CLIPS TYING HIM DOWN. THE SICKLY, ZOO-SMELL OF ODDJOB ENVELOPED HIM...

ODDJOB'S GRADE ONE MASSAGE IS HIGHLY PERSUASIVE...

GRADES TWO AND THREE, WHICH FOLLOW, EVEN MORE SO...

ALWAYS THE HARD HANDS WERE SURGICALLY ACCURATE. BOND GROUND HIS TEETH UNTIL HE THOUGHT THEY WOULD BREAK

Fu Manchu

From **Fu Manchu** By **Sax Rohmer (Arthur Henry Ward)**

'He wore a plain yellow robe, of a hue almost identical with that of his smooth, hairless countenance. His hands were large, long and bony, and he held them knuckles upward, and rested his pointed chin upon their thinness. He had a great high brow, crowned with sparse, neutral-coloured hair.

'Of his face as it looked out at me over the dirty table, I despair of writing convincingly. It was that of an archangel of evil, and it was wholly dominated by the most uncanny eyes that ever reflected a human soul, for they were narrow and long, very slightly oblique, and of a brilliant green. But their unique horror lay in a certain filminess (it made me think of the membrana nictitans in a bird) which, obscuring them as I threw aside the door, seemed to lift as I actually passed the threshold, revealing the eyes in all their brilliant viridescence.'
Sax Rohmer

The Story

Dr Fu Manchu is the diabolical agent of the Yellow Peril in Britain. He uses his scientific genius to plot mysterious and cruel deaths for those who might prove an obstruction to his plans to conquer the Western world and set up an Oriental Empire. His chief adversary in Britain is Nayland Smith, who returns unexpectedly from his government post in Burma to take up the fight against the 'Lord of Strange Deaths'.

The contest between Oriental cunning and British grit proves a well matched one, and Nayland Smith, with his friend, Doctor Petrie, escape death many times from the hands of the mysterious Chinaman. Dr Fu Manchu is an elusive quarry, and in spite of the efforts of Smith and Petrie, remains free to continue his grim fight.

In 1911, having been commissioned by a magazine to write an article on Limehouse, Sax Rohmer found himself on the trail of a 'Mr King', supposedly mastermind of half the Chinatown underworld. During his investigations an idea began to form in his mind. The creation of a character for a novel based on the elusive 'Mr King'. The article was finished without a sight of him, but Sax Rohmer returned to Limehouse to continue the trail. Acting upon information received from Fong Wah, an old and respected Chinaman, who kept a shop in Limehouse, Rohmer staged a night-time vigil outside a house in Three Colt Street, near the Limehouse Cut. His reward was a glimpse of the mysterious tall, dignified Chinaman alighting from a limousine, followed by a beautiful Arabian girl. He never discovered if the Chinaman was 'Mr King', or not, but he knew instantly that he had seen the face he had been searching for—the face of his newly created arch-villain—the face of Fu Manchu.

Fu Manchu on film

1923 Stoll
The Mystery of Fu Manchu
(15-part serial), Harry Agar Lyons

1924 Stoll
The Further Mysteries of Fu Manchu
Harry Agar Lyons

1929 Paramount
The Mysterious Doctor Fu Manchu
Werner Oland

1930 Paramount
The Return of Doctor Fu Manchu (also called
The New Adventures of Dr Fu Manchu)
Werner Oland

1930 Paramount
Daughter of the Dragon
Werner Oland

1932 MGM
The Mask of Fu Manchu
Boris Karloff

1940 Republic
Drums of Fu Manchu
(15-part serial later made into a 68-minute
feature. Released 1943)

1948 *El Otro Fu Manchu (The Other Fu Manchu)*
(Spain)
Manuel Requena

1950 NBC
(There was to have been a TV series, but
only the pilot was made as the sponsors were
disappointed with the script)

1955 Republic
The Adventures of Fu Manchu
Glen Gordon
(Republic bought the TV, Radio and Film
rights from Sax Rohmer for $4 million and
developed a TV series with 78 half-hour
instalments. Only 13 were shown)

1965 Seven Arts
The Face of Fu Manchu
Christopher Lee

Boris Karloff in the 1930 screen version of *The Mask of Fu Manchu*.

(The first Fu Manchu film made in colour. Filmed as a series. Originally entitled *The Mask of Fu Manchu*)

1966 Seven Arts
The Brides of Fu Manchu
Christopher Lee

1967 Warner Bros. Seven Arts
The Vengeance of Fu Manchu
Christopher Lee

1968 English Towers
Assignment Istanbul
Christopher Lee
(Originally entitled *The Castle of Fu Manchu*)

1969 English Towers
Kiss and Kill
Christopher Lee
(Originally entitled *The Blood of Fu Manchu* in the USA
and *Fu Manchu and the Kiss of Death* in UK.)

Fu Manchu in the theatre

Although Fu Manchu has appeared on film, TV and radio, two attempts by Sax Rohmer at a stage adaptation were unsuccessful, and it has never appeared in the theatre.

Fu Manchu in print

1912 (Published as a serialisation in the magazine 'The Story Teller' (England)

1913 (Published as a serialisation in the magazine 'Collier's Weekly' (USA)

1913 *The Mystery of Dr. Fu-Manchu*. Methuen (London), (title in USA: *The Insidious Dr Fu-Manchu*)

1916 *The Devil Doctor*. Methuen (London) (in USA as *The Return of Dr Fu Manchu*, McBride (New York)

1917 *The Si-Fan Mysteries*. Methuen (London) (in USA as *The Hand of Fu Manchu*). McBride (New York)

1929 *The Book of Fu Manchu* (Omnibus). Hurst and Blackett (London). McBride (New York)

1931 *Daughter of Fu Manchu*. The Crime Club (New York)

1931 Daughter of Fu Manchu. Cassell (London)

1932 *The Mask of Fu Manchu*. The Crime Club (New York)

1933 *The Mask of Fu Manchu*. Cassell (London)

1933 *Fu Manchu's Bride*. The Crime Club (New York)
(Published in UK as *The Bride of Fu Manchu* Cassell (London))

1934 *The Trail of Fu Manchu*. The Crime Club (New York)

1934 *The Trail of Fu Manchu*. Cassell (London)

1936 *President Fu Manchu*. The Crime Club (New York)

1936 *President Fu Manchu*. Cassell (London)

1939 *The Drums of Fu Manchu*. The Crime Club (New York)

1939 *The Drums of Fu Manchu*. Cassell (London)

1941 *The Island of Fu Manchu*. The Crime Club (New York)

1941 *The Island of Fu Manchu*. Cassell (London)

1948 *The Shadow of Fu Manchu*. The Crime Club (New York)

1949 *The Shadow of Fu Manchu*. Herbert Jenkins (London)

1957 *Re-enter Fu Manchu*. Gold Medal Books (Connecticut)
(Published in UK under the title *Re-enter Dr. Fu Manchu*. Herbert Jenkins (London))

1959 *Emperor Fu Manchu*. Herbert Jenkins (London)

1959 *Emperor Fu Manchu*. Gold Medal Books (Connecticut)

After the first three books of Fu Manchu the hyphen in the name was dropped.
The Crime Club novels were published by Doubleday, Doran & Co (later Doubleday & Co)

Christopher Lee as Fu Manchu.

Christopher Lee and Tsai Chin in the 1965 screen version of *The Face of Fu Manchu*.

Werner Oland in the 1929 screen version of *The Mysterious Dr Fu Manchu*.

Carl Peterson

From **Bulldog Drummond** By **Sapper** (H. C. McNeile)

' "He is about medium height and rather thick set; clean shaven, with thick brown hair flecked slightly with white. His forehead is broad, and his eyes are a sort of cold grey blue. But it's his hands that terrify me. They're large and white and utterly ruthless." She turned to him appealingly, "Oh, don't think I'm talking wildly," she implored. "He frightens me to death—that man; far worse than Lakington. He would stop at nothing to gain his ends, and even Lakington himself knows that Mr Peterson is master." '
Sapper

The Story

The aim of arch-criminal and master-mind Carl Peterson (alias the Comte de Guy, alias Edward Blackton, alias Mr Wilmot) is to bring about the downfall of England for his own gain. But his efforts are continuously thwarted by the intervention of Captain Hugh 'Bulldog' Drummond, DSO, MC, whose brave band of dare-devil Englishmen easily outwit and outfight Carl Peterson's rascally gang of foreigners and bolshevists. But Peterson himself continues to elude Drummond until the

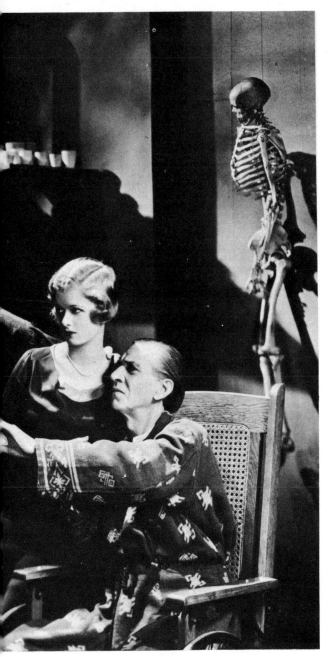

The Background

Sapper stated on the radio programme 'In Town Tonight' that he had modelled Drummond on Gerard Fairlie. When asked if Peterson, Irma and the rest were based on originals he replied, 'Sometimes'. In fact Sapper has been remarkably reticent about Peterson. He never appears twice with the same identity—or even the same nationality. His private life begins and ends, it seems, with his mistress, Irma.

We are never told who Irma is, on the death of Peterson she swears to continue the fight against Drummond, but neither Sapper, nor Gerard Fairlie, who took over the writing of the Drummond books from Sapper, saw fit to shed any more light on her.

What was Peterson's real name? Even Irma is never heard to use it.

Why did Peterson and Irma never marry? was one (or both) of them married already or did they just prefer it that way?

And for whom did Peterson work? For Peterson, seems to be the short answer. But mention is made of Drakshoff for whom (for five million pounds) Peterson has stopped a revolution. It is Peterson's versatility, elusiveness, and inscrutability that make him a fascinating and worthy match for Bulldog Drummond. In fact there is a slight but persistent feeling that he is wasted on him.

Bulldog Drummond on film

1922   Hollandia Film Corporation
       Bulldog Drummond
       Starring Evelyn Greeley

1925   Astra National/Capital Productions
       Bulldog Drummond's Third Round
       Drummond (Jack Buchanan)

1929   Goldwyn / United Artists
       (adapted from the Du Maurier stage
       production)
       Drummond (Ronald Colman)
       Carl Peterson (Montague Love)

Bulldog Drummond in the theatre

1921   Wyndham's Theatre
       A play by Sapper
       Peterson (Alfred Drayton)

Bulldog Drummond in print

A selected list of publications featuring Carl Peterson

1921   *Bulldog Drummond*

1926   *The Final Count*. Hodder & Stoughton
       (London)

1929   *His Four Rounds with Carl Peterson.*
       (*Bulldog Drummond, The Black Gang, The
       Third Round, The Final Count*)

1933   *The Black Gang*

1950   *Bulldog Drummond*. Brockhampton Press

summer of 1927 when his plot for mass destruction by dropping a lethal poison from the air is foiled by the intrepid Captain who, with his customary ingenuity and iron nerve, turns the poison to Peterson's own destruction. After his death, Peterson's mistress, Irma, vows revenge on Captain Drummond.

Peter Quint

From **The Turn of the Screw** By **Henry James**

An illustration by Mariette Lydis of Peter Quint from the 1940 edition of *The Turn of the Screw*.

'He has red hair, very red, close curling, and a pale face, long in shape, with straight good features and little rather queer whiskers that are as red as his hair. His eyebrows are somehow darker; they look particularly arched and as if they might move a great deal. His eyes are sharp, strange—awfully; but I only know clearly that they are rather small and very fixed. His mouth's wide and his lips are thin, and except for his little whiskers he's quite clean shaven. He gives me a sort of sense of looking like an actor'
Henry James

Marlon Brando as Peter Quint in the 1972 screen version of *The Turn of the Screw* retitled *The Nightcomers*.

The Story

Peter Quint, valet to a rich bachelor, lived, because of his health, in his employer's country house, Bly, in Essex. Having insinuated himself into a position of trust, he was given charge of the estate and the two children, Flora and Miles, the wards of his employer. His influence was an evil one. He seduced the Governess, Miss Jessell, and the pair exerted a sinister hold on the two children. One morning Quint was found dead in the road with a wound on his head. It was presumed that he was drunk and had slipped on the icy road. At the inquest his many vices were uncovered. Miss Jessell left Bly and later died also.

The new Governess is haunted by apparitions of Peter Quint and Miss Jessell. She becomes obsessed with the idea that their evil spirits are corrupting Flora and Miles from the grave. Her attempts to free the children from their unholy influence leads to the collapse of Flora and the death of Miles.

The Background

Whether the evil manifestations which appeared in the house at Bly were real or the imaginings of an over-sensitive and sexually repressed woman has been a point of controversy amongst critics and scholars since the first appearance of *Turn of the Screw*. In letters to Dr Louis Waldstein and H. G. Wells in 1898, James modestly disclaimed the exaggerated significance read into what he refers to as his 'pot boiler'. To F. W. H. Myers, 19 December 1898, he wrote:

'... the *Turn of the Screw* is a very mechanical matter, I honestly think, an inferior, a merely pictorial subject, and rather a shameless pot boiler. The thing that, as I recall it, I most wanted not to fail of doing, under penalty of extreme platitude, was to give the impression of the communication to the children of the most infernal imaginable evil and danger—the condition on their part, of being as exposed as we can humanly conceive children to be. This was my artistic knot to untie, to put any sense or logic in the thing, and if I had known any sense of producing more the image of their contact and condition I should assuredly have been proportionately eager to resort to it. I evoked the worst I could, and only feel tempted to say, as in French; 'Excusez du peu".'

Turn of the Screw on film

1961 20th Century Fox
Re-titled *The Innocents*
Peter Quint (Peter Wyngarde)

1972 Joseph Levine/Avco Embassy
Re-titled *The Nightcomers*
Peter Quint (Marlon Brando)

Turn of the Screw in the theatre

1946 Arts Theatre, London
Dramatisation by Allan Turpin

1953 Aldeburgh Festival
Opera *Turn of the Screw*
Music by Benjamin Britten
Adaptation by Myfanwy Piper
Vocal Score by Imogen Holst
Peter Quint (Peter Pears)
(subsequently at the Sadler's Wells Theatre, 1954)

Turn of the Screw in print

(*A selected list*)

Serialised in *Collier's Weekly*, 5 February to 6 April 1898

1898 Heinemann (London)

1940 Hand and Flower Press (London), illustrated by Mariette Lydis

1946 Penguin (Harmondsworth)

1950 Coward McCann (New York), play by Wm. Archibald, *The Innocents* (based on *The Turn of the Screw*), drawings by the Author

1951 Samuel French (London)

1957 Harold C. Goddard (Nineteenth Century Fiction, volume 12, no. I), 'A pre-Freudian reading of *The Turn of the Screw*

1960 Thos. Y. Crowell & Co. (New York), *A casebook on Henry James Turn of the Screw* by various authors (Crowell Literary Casebooks)

1965 Thos. M. Cranfill & R. L. Clark (New York) *An anatomy of The Turn of the Screw*

1967 Oxford University Press (Oxford)

The Marquis de St Evremonde

From **A Tale of Two Cities** By **Charles Dickens**

'He was a man of about sixty, handsomely dressed, haughty in manner, and with a face like a fine mask. A face of transparent paleness; every feature in it clearly defined; one set expression on it. The nose, beautifully formed otherwise, was very slightly pinched at the top of each nostril. In those two compressions, or dints, the only little change that the face ever showed, resided. They persisted in changing colour sometimes, and they would be occasionally dilated and contracted by something like a faint pulsation, then they gave a look of treachery and cruelty, to the whole countenance. Examined with attention, its capacity of helping such a look was to be found in the line of the mouth, and the lines of the orbits of the eyes, being much too horizontal and thin; still, in the effect the face made it was a handsome face, and a remarkable one.'

Charles Dickens

The Story

The village accepts as normal their suffering under the oppressive rule of the landowner, the Marquis de St Evremonde. The brother of the Marquis asks to be given one of the village girls. The girl and her husband refuse to subject themselves to him. Using their feudal rights the St Evremondes work the husband until he drops dead. St Evremonde's brother rapes the girl, she loses her mind and dies. Her brother, seeking revenge, fights St Evremonde's brother and is killed. Some years later the Marquis's coach runs over a child and kills it. That night he is murdered. When the French revolution breaks out the revenge of Madame Defarge, the sister of St Evremonde's rape victim, falls upon Charles Darnay, the surviving member of the St Evremonde family who years before had relinquished his claim to the title.

Basil Rathbone as D'Evremonde in the 1935 screen version of *A Tale of Two Cities*.

An illustration by H. K. Browne (Phiz) from the 1859 edition of *A Tale of Two Cities*.

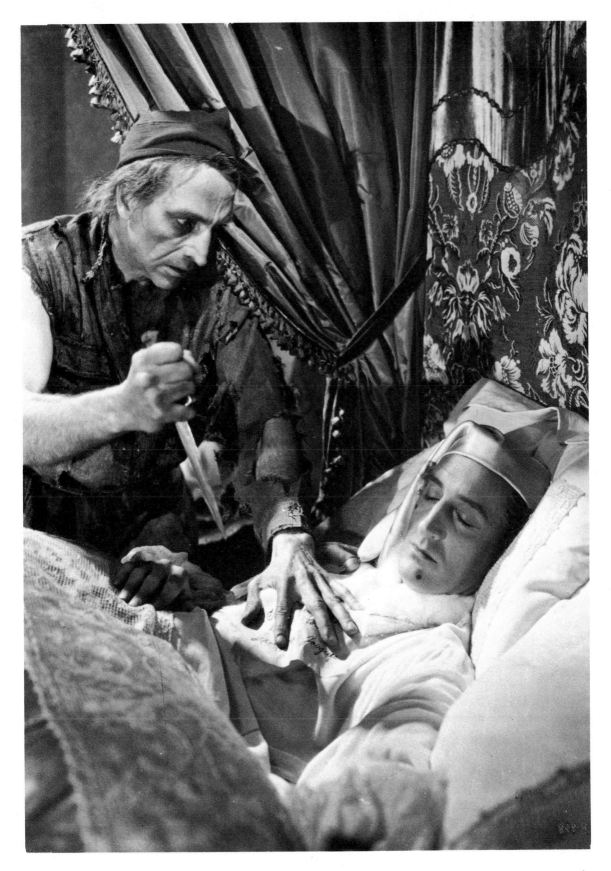

The Background

A Tale of Two Cities was written during a period of great stress in Dickens' life just after his parting from his wife. 'If I can discipline my thoughts into the channel of a story, I have made up my mind to get to work on one', he wrote. He determined to produce something different in style from his usual work—a story of incident with characters expressed through the action of the tale rather than the dialogue. His great admiration for Carlyle, and sympathy with the oppressed people of the French Revolution inspired the setting of his book:

'Whenever any reference, however slight, is made here to the condition of the French people before or during the Revolution, it is truly made, on the faith of trustworthy witnesses. It has been one of my hopes to add something to the popular and picturesque means of understanding that terrible time, though no one can hope to add anything to the philosophy of Mr Carlyle's wonderful book.'

A Tale of Two Cities on film

1911   Vitagraph
Director James Stuart Blackton
Carton (Maurice Costello)
D'Evremonde (William Humphreys)

1917   William Fox Studios
Director Frank Lloyd
Carton (Willian Farnum)
D'Evremonde (Charles Clary)

1925   Herbert Wilcox Production
The Only Way
Carton (Martin Harvey)
D'Evremonde (Ben Webster)

1935   Selznick/MGM
Carton (Ronald Colman)
D'Evremonde (Basil Rathbone)

1957   Betty Box/Ralph Thomas
(Distributed by Rank)
Carton (Dirk Bogarde)
D'Evremonde (Christopher Lee)

Christopher Lee as D'Evremonde in the 1957 screen version of *A Tale of Two Cities*.

A Tale of Two Cities in the theatre

1860   The Lyceum Theatre
Play by Tom Taylor from Dickens' story
D'Evremond (Acton Bond)

1899   *The Only Way*
by Revd. Freeman Willis
and Frederick Langbridge

A Tale of Two Cities in print

(A selected list)

First serialised in the magazine *All the Year Round*

1859   Chapman and Hall (London), illustrated by
H. K. Browne (Phiz)

1859   J. B. Peterson & Bros (Philadelphia), illustrated by John McLennan

1866   Chapman and Hall (London)

1889   Chapman and Hall (London) (frontispiece by
Fred Barnard), with details of the Lyceum
Theatre production

1902   James Nisbet & Co, illustrated by F. H.
Townsend

1906   John Lang, illustrated by F. Chesworth

1910   Chapman and Hall (London), illustrated by
S. E. Scott

1925   G. G. Harrap & Co (London), illustrated by
Rowland Wheelwright

1934   Macmillan & Co (London), introduction by
G. K. Chesterton

1949   Collins (London), illustrated by Harry Keen

1952   The Folio Society (London), drawings by
Richard Sharp

1958   Longmans, Green & Co (London), introduction and notes by S. H. Burton

1962   Macmillan (New York/London), illustrated by
R. M. Powers (afterwards Clifton Fardiman)

1966   Blackie & Son (London and Glasgow), introduction and notes by A. R. Tomkins

A Tale of Two Cities has been translated into:
Arabic, Danish, Dutch, Finnish, French, Hebrew,
Irish, Italian, Punjabi, Russian, Spanish, Tamil.

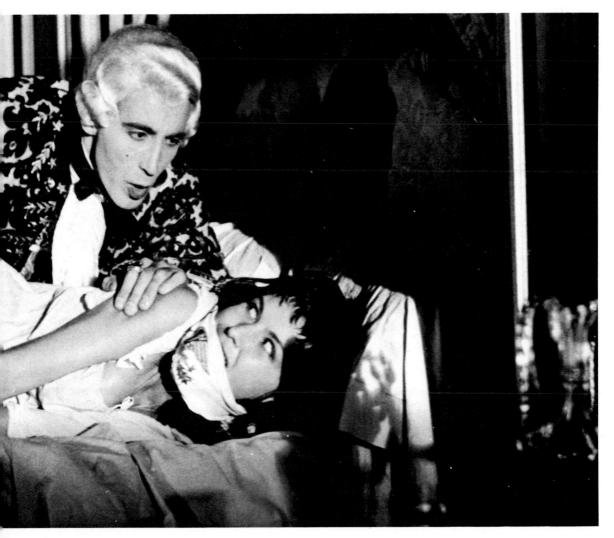

Injun Joe

From **The Adventures of Tom Sawyer** By **Mark Twain (Samuel Langhorne Clemens)**

' "... Yes, and you done more than that", said Injun Joe, approaching the doctor, who was now standing. "Five years ago you drove me away from your father's kitchen one night, when I come to ask for something to eat, and you said I wasn't there for any good; and when I swore I'd get even with you if it took a hundred years, your father had me jailed for a vagrant. Did you think I'd forget? The Injun blood ain't in me for nothing. And now I've *got* you, and you got to settle, you know!"

'... the doctor struck out suddenly and stretched the ruffian to the ground. Potter dropped his knife and exclaimed "Here, now, don't you hit my pard!" ...

'... Injun Joe sprang to his feet, his eyes flaming with passion, snatched up Potter's knife, and went creeping catlike and stooping, round and round about the combatants seeking an opportunity. All at once the doctor flung himself free ... felled Potter to the earth ... in the same instant the half-breed saw his chance, and drove the knife to the hilt in the young man's breast ...

'... presently the moon emerged again ... the half-breed muttered: "That score is settled, damn you!" Then he robbed the body. After which he put the fatal knife in Potter's open right hand, and sat down on the dismantled coffin. ...'
Mark Twain

The Story

When Injun Joe, the half-breed, begged food from the house of young Doctor Robinson, the doctor's father had him jailed for vagrancy and Mr Douglas, the Justice of the Peace, had him horse-whipped publicly. Injun Joe swore revenge. Five years later he and Muff Potter, a harmless, befuddled old drunk, are body snatching with Dr Robinson. A fight breaks out, Potter is knocked senseless, and Injun Joe, seeing the opportunity for revenge, stabs the doctor. He plants the knife on the unconscious Potter and when he wakes accuses him of the murder. Tom Sawyer, hidden in the graveyard, has witnessed the murder, and at the trial of Potter Tom denounces Injun Joe. Potter is cleared and Injun Joe escapes through a court-room window. With an accomplice he goes into hiding disguised as a deaf and dumb Spaniard. They find a fortune hidden under the floor boards of an old house. Injun plans to hide it, complete his revenge on the widow of Mr Douglas, and escape to Texas. But the two men have been overheard by Tom and his friend Huckleberry Finn. Some days later, whilst on a picnic Tom is lost exploring the caves with his friend Becky Thatcher. Whilst he is missing Huck tracks down Injun Joe, and hears him plotting with his accomplice to attack the Widow Douglas. Huck sets up the alarm and the men are chased from the town. Injun Joe flees to McDougal's cave where he hides the treasure. Tom and Becky, still lost in the cave, see Injun Joe, but manage to escape before Injun Joe realises that they are there. As a result of Tom and Becky's adventure the cave is sealed to prevent anyone else getting lost. Tom realises that Injun Joe is still inside, but by the time the search party reaches him he is dead.

The Background

Injun Joe, a half-breed and local drunk, lived in the American mid-west town of Hannibal, the boyhood home of Samuel Langhorne Clemens, which when he adopted the pseudonym of Mark Twain, became the setting for the *Adventures of Tom Sawyer*.

'Little Sam's' father had attempted to reform Injun Joe ... it was a failure and we boys were glad. For Injun Joe was interesting and a bene-faction to us, but Injun Joe was a dreary spectacle. We watched my father's experiments on him with a

good deal of anxiety, but it came out all right, and we were satisfied. Injun Joe got drunk oftener than before, and became intolerably interesting.

Three miles below Hannibal was a great cave. It was miles in extent and was a tangled wilderness of narrow and lofty clefts and passages. It was an easy place to get lost in; anybody could do it—including the bats. Once Injun Joe was lost down there. He managed to survive on a diet of bats until he was rescued. Later he recounted his experiences to 'Little Sam'. 'Little Sam' never forgot and years later, as Mark Twain, recalled his experience in the *Adventures of Tom Sawyer*—but with a difference: Mark Twain's Injun Joe died in the caves. 'Little Joe' never knew how his Injun Joe died, but he knew when. 'The news of Injun Joe's death reached me at a most unhappy time—that is to say, just at bedtime on a summer night, when a prodigious storm of thunder and lightning, accompanied by a deluging rain that turned the streets and lanes into rivers, caused me to repent and resolve to lead a better life. I can remember the awful thunder bursts and the white glare of lightning yet, and the wild lashing of the rain against the window panes. By my teaching I knew perfectly well what all the rumpus was for—Satan had come to get Injun Joe. . . .'

Tom Sawyer on film

1917   A Paramount Production
       Tom Sawyer (Jack Pickford)
       (The part of Injun Joe was cut, along with all the other 'less pleasant' moments)

1930   Paramount
       Tom Sawyer (Jackie Coogan)
       Injun Joe (Charles Stevens)

1938   Selznick/United Artists
       Tom Sawyer (Tommy Kelly)
       Injun Joe (Victor Jory)

1969   Film Studio Bucuresti/Franco London Films
       Abentuville Lai Tom Sawyer
       A Rumanian/French Production.

1973   Readers Digest/United Artists
       Produced by Frank Capra
       Injun Joe (Kunu Hank)

1973   CBS Television Production

Tom Sawyer in print

(*A selected list*)

1876   American Publishing Co (Hartford, Connecticut), illustrated

1876   Chatto & Windus (London)

1902   Poole Stewart Publishing Co (Toronto), illustrated by D. F. Thomson

1911   Chatto & Windus, illustrated by Worth Brehm

1936   T. Nelson & Sons (London), illustrated by A. S. Forrest

1950   Puffin (Harmondsworth)

1951   Blackie & Sons (London & Glasgow), illustrated by Raymond Sheppard

1955   J. M. Dent & Sons (London), E. P. Dutton & Co (New York), illustrated by C. Walter Hodges

1962   Macmillan & Co (London), illustrated by John Falter, 'after word by Clifton Fadiman'

Tom Sawyer's dream of Injun Joe from the 1876 edition of the book.

The Joker

From **Batman**

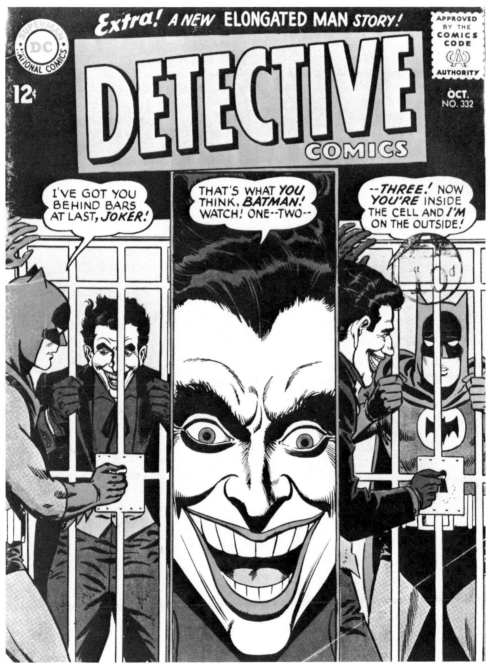

Cover for Detective Comics

Every Super Hero must have a super villain to exercise his brain and muscle power and keep him on his toes. Dr Doom is pitted against Richard Reed (Mr Fantastic), The Red Skull against Captain America, Superman has coped with two major villains—Lex Luther and Brainiac. But when it comes to Batman and Robin the balance is disturbed. Does it take *two* super-goodies to vanquish a super 'baddie'? Not in the least. The Caped Crusaders are faced with *several* super baddies. The Riddler, Mr Penguin, King Tut, Mr Freeze and the Cat Woman, to name but a few. And although they may not attack *en masse* they seem to follow in pretty quick rotation, leaving the Dynamic Duo very little time in which to take a super breather.

King of Batman and Robin's baddies is that jesting jackanapes The Joker! Well may the law-abiding citizens of Gotham City tremble when the comic of crime is at large. The abnormal appearance of the Dynamic Duo's ace adversary, green hair, white face and vivid red lips, is the result of a chemical reaction. The Joker always strikes at the world through Gotham City where Batman and Robin (alias millionaire Bruce Wayne and his ward, Dick Grayson) wage their tireless war on crime from their secret bat cave under stately Wayne Manor.

The Joker's schemes to wisecrack his way to defeating Batman and the Boy Wonder have not so far succeeded—although he has come close. But to quote Batman himself, 'Close doesn't count'.

The Background

Batman, Robin and their oddly assorted adversaries first appeared in comic form in 1939 in 'Detective Comics', published and distributed by National Periodical Publications. Sparta (Illinois) and New York.
The creators were Bob Kane and Bill Finger.
Later they were promoted to their own magazine in April 1940, when the first 'Batman' comic appeared.

Cesar Romero as The Joker in the 1960 screen version of *Batman*.

Batman on film

1943   Serial version by Columbia Pictures in association with National Periodical Publications.
Batman (Lewis Willson)
(The Joker not featured)

1950   Serial version
Columbia Pictures
Batman (Robert Lowery)

1960s   TV Series, eventually made into a full-length feature film (Greenway Prods. Dist. 20th Century Fox)
Batman (Adam West)
Joker (Cesar Romero)
(In 1974 this series enjoyed a new lease of life when it was reshown in the Saturday morning children's programme *Saturday Scene* on London Weekend Television)

The Batman newspaper cartoon strip was discontinued in 1946, but revived for a short time in the 1960s.

Lady Macbeth

From **Macbeth** By **William Shakespeare**

'Come, you spirits,
That tend on mortal thoughts, unsex me here;
And fill me, from the crown to the toe, top full
Of direst cruelty. Make thick my blood,
Stop. up th'access and passage to remorse,
That no compunctious visitings of nature
Shake my fell purpose nor keep peace between
Th' effect and it . . .
Lady Macbeth—William Shakespeare

The Story

It is foretold to Macbeth, thane of Glamis, by three
witches that he will become King of Scotland,
although his children will not succeed to the throne.
Lady Macbeth, a woman of apparent charm and self
possession, stronger willed than her husband and
ruthlessly ambitious for him, forces him into the
murder of King Duncan. Duncan's sons, Malcolm
and Donalbain, escape and flee the country and
Macbeth is crowned King. Remembering the
witches prediction and fearing for the succession of
their children, the newly crowned King and Queen
brutally murder any would-be contenders for the
throne. Hearing that Malcolm is forming an army
to march on him, Macbeth leaves to rally his troops.
While he is away, the Queen, gradually overcome
by her guilt, takes her life shortly before her husband is killed in battle.

**Isuzo Yamada as Asji (Lady Macbeth) in *Throne of
Blood,* the 1957 screen version.**

Ellen Terry as Lady Macbeth.

The Background

Gruoch, Lady Macbeth, daughter of Bodhe, and direct descendant of Kenneth III, was originally married to Gillacomgan who succeeded Finlag, father of Macbeth, as Mormaer of Moray, until 1032, when he was burnt to death in a skirmish with the Southern reigning house. She then married Macbeth who himself became the Mormaer of Moray. Macbeth's claim to the throne of Scotland was a strong one through his mother back to Kenneth II. Malcolm II, contrary to the usual rule, was anxious that his grandson, Duncan, should succeed him, and through his machinations Duncan became king on 25 November 1034. On 14 August 1040, Macbeth killed him at Bothnagown, near Elgin. Gruoch and Macbeth became King and Queen of Scotland. Their reign is said to have been a good and popular one. In 1050 they made a pilgrimage to Rome where they distributed money to the poor. Norman fugitives from England were sheltered by them in 1052. Macbeth was killed at Lumphannan in Mar, on 15 August 1057, aged about 52, by Malcolm King of the Cumbrians (afterwards Malcolm III). Macbeth and Gruoch had no children. They reigned for 17 years and 2 days. Macbeth was succeeded by Lulach, Gruoch's son by Gillacomgan, who was slain by Malcolm after reigning for only 7 months.

Lady Macbeth on film

1908 Vitagraph
      Directed by William V. Ranous
      Lady Macbeth (Miss Carver)

1909 Cines of Rome

1910 Film D'Art/Pathe
      Directed by Andre Calmettes
      Lady Macbeth (Jeanne Delvair)

1911 Co-Operative
      Lady Macbeth (Mrs F. R. Benson)

1913 Film Industrie Gesellschaft
      Lady Macbeth (Violet Vanburgh)

1914 Burlesque version originally scripted and
      directed by James Barrie, entitled *The Real
      Thing at Last*
      Produced by A. E. Matthews
      Lady Macbeth (Nelson Keyes)

1916 Eclair Films
      Lady Macbeth (Madame Georgette Leblanc
      Maeterlinck)

1916 Triangle Reliance
      Macbeth (Sir Herbert Beerbohm Tree)
      Lady Macbeth (Constance Collier)

1922 Elel-Film (Germany)

1948 Republic Pictures/Mercury Films
      Lady Macbeth (Jeanette Nolan)
      Macbeth (Orson Welles)

1960 Grand Prize Films
Lady Macbeth (Judith Anderson)
Macbeth (Maurice Evans)

1957 Japan-Toho Production
Directed by Akira Kurosawa
Asji—Lady Macbeth (Isuzu Yamada)
Entitled *The Throne of Blood*
The Castle of the Spider's Web

Lady Macbeth in the theatre

1610 The Globe

Possibly performed four years previously.
This suggested by an allusion in Act 4, Scene
1, to the union of the three kingdoms
England, Ireland and Scotland in the hands of
James 1, who ascended the throne in 1602–3
and was proclaimed king of all three in 1604.

1672 Dorset Garden
Lady Macbeth (Mrs Betterton)

1707 The Haymarket
Lady Macbeth (Mrs Barry)

1711 Drury Lane
Lady Macbeth (Mrs Knight)

1717 Drury Lane
Lady Macbeth (Mrs Porter)

1723 Lincoln's Inn Fields
Lady Macbeth (Mrs McKnight)

1733 Covent Garden
Lady Macbeth (Mrs Hallam)

1744 Drury Lane
Lady Macbeth (Mrs Giffard)

1746 Drury Lane
Lady Macbeth (Mrs Macklin)

1748 Drury Lane
Lady Macbeth (Mrs Pritchard)

1754 Covent Garden
Lady Macbeth (Peg Woffington)

1768 Covent Garden
Lady Macbeth (Mrs Yates)

1770 Drury Lane
Lady Macbeth (Mrs Barry)

1773 Covent Garden

1778 The Haymarket
Lady Macbeth (Mrs Massey)

1780 Drury Lane
Lady Macbeth (Mrs Crawford)

1785 Drury Lane
Lady Macbeth (Mrs. Siddons)

1794 Drury Lane
Lady Macbeth (Mrs Siddons)

1800 Covent Garden
Lady Macbeth (Mrs Litchfield)

1814 Drury Lane
Lady Macbeth (Mrs Bartley)

1820 Covent Garden
Lady Macbeth (Mrs Bunn)

1831 Drury Lane
Lady Macbeth (Miss Huddart)

1832 Covent Garden
Lady Macbeth (Fanny Kemble)

Lady Macbeth drawn by Salvador Dali.

1834 Covent Garden
Lady Macbeth (Miss Clifton)

1835 Drury Lane
Lady Macbeth (Ellen Tree)

1835 Covent Garden Theatre
Lady Macbeth (Mrs W. West)

1836 Drury Lane Theatre
Lady Macbeth (Miss Huddart)

1842 Haymarket Theatre
Lady Macbeth (Mrs Charles Kean)

1844 Sadler's Wells Theatre
Lady Macbeth (Mrs Warner)

1845 Princess's Theatre
Lady Macbeth (Charlotte Cushman)

1846 Princess's Theatre
Lady Macbeth (Charlotte Cushman)

1848 Olympic Theatre
Lady Macbeth (Isabella Glyn)

1848 Princess's Theatre
Lady Macbeth (Fanny Kemble)

1850 Sadler's Wells Theatre
Lady Macbeth (Miss Glyn)

1853	Princess's Theatre Lady Macbeth (Mrs Charles Kean)
1853	Marylebone Theatre Lady Macbeth (Mrs J. W. Wallack)
1855	Drury Lane Theatre Lady Macbeth (Mrs J. W. Wallack)
1858	Lyceum Theatre Lady Macbeth (Helen Faucit)
1866	Drury Lane Theatre Lady Macbeth (Amy Sedgwick)
1867	Drury Lane Theatre Lady Macbeth (Mrs Hermann Vezin)
1875	Lyceum Theatre Lady Macbeth (Kate Bateman)
1876	Drury Lane Theatre Lady Macbeth (Genevieve Ward)
1882	Drury Lane Theatre Lady Macbeth (Madame Ristori)
1888	Olympic Theatre Lady Macbeth (Mrs Bandman Palmer)
1888	Lyceum Theatre Lady Macbeth (Ellen Terry)
1895	Lyceum Theatre Lady Macbeth (Ellen Terry)
1898	Lyceum Theatre Lady Macbeth (Mrs Patrick Campbell)
1906	Garrick Theatre Lady Macbeth (Violet Vanburgh)
1909	His Majesty's Theatre Lady Macbeth (Violet Vanburgh)
1911	His Majesty's Theatre Lady Macbeth (Violet Vanburgh)
1920	Aldwych Theatre Lady Macbeth (Mrs Patrick Campbell)
1926	The Old Vic Lady Macbeth (Dorothy Massingham)
1926	Princes Theatre Lady Macbeth (Sybil Thorndike)
1928	Court Theatre (In modern costume) Lady Macbeth (Mary Merrill)
1930	The Old Vic Lady Macbeth (Martita Hunt)
1932	Kingsway Theatre Lady Macbeth (Eileen Thorndike)
1932	The Old Vic Lady Macbeth (Margaret Webster)
1934	The Old Vic Lady Macbeth (Flora Robson)
1935	The Old Vic Lady Macbeth (Vivienne Bennett)
1937	The Old Vic Lady Macbeth (Judith Anderson)
1942	Piccadilly Lady Macbeth (Gwen Ffrangcon Davies)
1944	Lyric Hammersmith Lady Macbeth (Vivienne Bennett)
1945	Winter Garden Lady Macbeth (Patricia Jessel)

1947	Aldwych Lady Macbeth (Ena Burrill)
1950	The Arts Lady Macbeth (Margaret Rawlings)
1953	King's Hammersmith Lady Macbeth (Rosalind Iden)
1954	The Old Vic Lady Macbeth (Ann Todd)
1956	The Old Vic Lady Macbeth (Coral Browne)
1958	The Old Vic Lady Macbeth (Beatrix Lehmann)

Macbeth in print

(*A selected list*)

1623	Seven years after Shakespeare's death two of his friends and fellow actors Henry Condell and John Henimming gathered together a collection of thirty-six plays he had written. This has since been referred to as the First Folio Edition, and was followed by Second, Third and Fourth Folios, in 1632, 1663 and 1685 respectively. Plays were also published singly, and known as Quarto editions, due to their format. Nineteen of them during the course of Shakespeare's lifetime and a twentieth just before 1623.
1673	Printed for William Cademan (as acted at the Duke's Theatre)
1674	Printed for P. Chetwin (as acted at the Duke's Theatre), with alterations and additions by Sir William Davenant
1687	Printed for Henry Heningman (as acted at the Theatre Royal)
1710	Printed for J. Tonson (as acted at the Queen's Theatre)
1729	Printed for J. Tonson, A Tragedy (as it is now acted by Her Majesty's servants)
1758	R. & A. Foulis (Glasgow), according to Mr Pope's second edition
1778	A. Vanderhoek's widow, Goettingen (with notes by Dr Johnson and Mr Sleevens)
1780	Harrison & Co (as acted at the Theatres Royal in Drury Lane and Covent Garden), with a portrait of Mr Garrick as Macbeth
1862	J. Gordon (Edinburgh), with chapters of Hollinshed's *Histories of Scotland*, introduction and notes by W. S. Dalgleish
1888	Nassau Steam Press (as arranged for the stage by Henry Irving, music by Arthur Sullivan, The Lyceum Theatre 29 December 1888)
1898	Nassau Steam Press (as arranged by Forbes Robertson with plate portraits of principal characters)
1927	Pan Books (London), introduction by Sir Lewis Casson
1946	Doubleday & Co (New York), illustrated by Salvador Dali
1951	The Folio Society (London), designs by Michael Ayrton, edited by M. R. Ridley

Long John Silver

From **Treasure Island** By **Robert Louis Stevenson**

'As I was waiting, a man came out of a side room, and at a glance, I was sure it must be Long John. His left leg was cut off close by the hip, and under the left shoulder he carried a crutch, which he managed with wonderful dexterity hopping about upon it like a bird. He was very tall and strong, with a face as big as a ham—plain and pale, but intelligent and smiling.'
Robert Louis Stevenson

Robert Newton as Long John Silver in the 1950 Walt Disney production of *Treasure Island.*

The Story

Pirate and murderer Long John Silver has an easy charm which he uses to his own advantage, changing his loyalties whenever it suits him. He had sailed as quartermaster with the late Captain Flint when the notorious pirate had buried his plundered treasure on a lonely island—later killing the men who had helped him bury it. Years later the map of the island falls into the hands of the young boy Jim Hawkins, whose friends, Dr Livesey and Squire Trelawney arrange a voyage to search for the treasure. Silver, with his usual cunning, secures berths for himself and his cronies. Almost all of them were original members of Captain Flint's old crew. Once arrived at the island, Silver leads a mutiny against the Captain and the Squire. With a few loyal members behind them they escape to the island and continue to wage the battle against Silver and his men. During the subsequent fighting, most of Silver's men are killed, and when his hypocritical offer to strike a bargain with his enemies is rejected, the remainder of his men turn against Silver. He is rescued by his enemies who, having found the treasure with the help of Ben Gunn, an old castaway, prepare to take Silver back to England to stand trial. Silver appears to accept his fate, but on the journey back home, at a stop at a Mexican port to recruit new hands, he slips overboard with a bag of coins and is never seen or heard of again.

The Background

The story of *Treasure Island* was born one wild and windy Scottish afternoon, when, to amuse a bored schoolboy, Stevenson drew a map of an island and imagined the story to go with it. It was originally entitled *The Sea Cook* after the dominant character of Long John Silver. Stevenson wrote of him in an article headed 'My First Book' which appeared in *The Idler* in August 1894:

'. . . and then I had an idea,' he wrote, 'for Long John Silver, from which I promised myself funds of entertainment; to take an admired friend of mine. . ., to deprive him of all his finer qualities and higher graces of temperament, to leave him nothing but his strength, his courage, his quickness, and his magnificent geniality, and try to express these terms in the character of a raw tarpaulin. . . I was not a little proud of John Silver . . . and to this day rather admire that smooth and formidable adventurer.'

Treasure Island on film

1912   Edison
1918   Fox Film Company
(Juvenile Company with Frances Cappenter and Virginia Corbin)

1920   Jesse Lasky/Famous Players
1934   MGM
Long John Silver (Wallace Beery)
1950   Walt Disney
Long John Silver (Robert Newton)
1971   Russian version
Produced by Gorski Central Studio
Long John Silver (B. Andreyev)
1973   MGM/EMI
Towers of London Production
Long John Silver (Orson Welles)

Treasure Island in the theatre

Adapted from Robert Louis Stevenson's book by J. B. Fagin. Opened at the Strand theatre in 1922. 1959 adapted by Bernard Miles and Peter Cow. Opened at the Mermaid Theatre 1959.

Treasure Island in print

(A selected list)

October 1881–January 1882, serialised in the magazine *The Young Folks*

1883   Cassell & Co (London)
1885   Cassell & Co (London)
1899   Cassell & Co (London), illustrated by Walter Paget
1911   Cassell & Co (London), illustrated by John Cameron
1927   Ernest Benn, illustrated by Edmund Dulac
1928   Ginn & Co (Boston), edited with introduction by Frank Wilson Cheney Hersey
1928   Macmillan & Co (London), illustrated by H. M. Brock
1929   Oxford University Press (Oxford), illustrated by Rowland Hilder
1934   Frederick Muller (London), illustrated by M. S. Orr
1949   Eyre & Spottiswoode (London), illustrated by Mervyn Peake
1955   Whitman Publishing Co. (London), illustrated by Paul Frame
1963   The Folio Society (London), illustrated by Peter Roberson
1972   Hamlyn (Feltham), illustrated by Paul Durand

A drawing by Walter Paget of Long John Silver from the 1883 edition of the book.

Hindley Earnshaw

From **Wuthering Heights** By **Emily Brontë**

'He entered, vociferating oaths dreadful to hear; caught me in the act of stowing his son away in the kitchen cupboard. Hareton was impressed with the wholesome terror of encountering either his wild beast's fondness or his mad man's rage; for in one he ran a chance of being squeezed and kissed to death, and in the other of being flung into the fire or dashed against the wall; and the poor thing remained perfectly quiet wherever I chose to put him.

' "There, I've found it out at last!" cried Hindley, pulling me back by the skin of my neck, like a dog, "By heaven and hell, you've sworn between you to murder that child! I know how it is now, that he is always out of my way. But with the help of Satan, I shall make you swallow the carving knife, Nelly! You needn't laugh; for I've just crammed Kenneth, head down most, in the Black horse marsh, and two is the same as one—and I want to kill some of you; I shall have no rest till I do!'

Emily Brontë

The Story

On the wild Yorkshire moors Hindley and Catherine Earnshaw grow up on their father's farm, Wuthering Heights. When Mr Earnshaw brings home an abandoned child, Cathy and Hindley have an immediate jealous hatred for it. It is christened Heathcliff and becomes Mr Earnshaw's favourite child. As they grow older Heathcliff and Cathy become inseparable but the bitter rivalry between Hindley and Heathcliff increases. After Mrs Earnshaw dies Hindley is sent to college. While he is away his father also dies. Hindley, now head of the family, returns with a wife, Frances, on whom he lavishes all his attention. When she shows a dislike of Heathcliff he is banished to the servants quarters and made to work as a labourer. Heathcliff swears revenge on him. Frances dies of consumption, leaving Hindley with a son, Hareton. He turns to drink, his dissipated life drives away all but two of the servants and demoralises his child whom he sometimes attacks during his bouts of drunken violence. Wuthering Heights becomes a desolate and comfortless house. When Cathy marries Edgar Linton of Thrushcross Grange, Heathcliff disappears. He returns a rich man and marries Edgar's sister Isabella. Hindley plays cards with him, loses, and mortgages Wuthering Heights to him. He dies of drink leaving Hareton disinherited and at the mercy of a man who hates him for his father's sake.

The Background

Most of the men who pick up a glass in a Brontë novel, are at one time or another, said to be modelled on Patrick Bramwell Brontë. Hindley, brother of Cathy, drinks himself into permanent oblivion after the death of his wife. Bramwell, brother of Emily, turned to drink after an abortive love affair. Hindley could indeed be Emily's portrait of her brother. It is only fair to Bramwell, however, to remember that most of the accusations against him, ranging from homosexuality to drug taking, and the oft repeated belief that he was the stumbling block in the way of his sisters' collective genius (he was not lacking in talent himself) are based on hearsay and speculation. Certainly he seems to have been an unstable, unhappy and frustrated boy, but living in the wilds of the Yorkshire moors, with only an aunt, an indifferent father, and three weird sisters for company could not have been good for a growing lad. His drinking did not kill him, he died of consumption—very likely helped along by his early Spartan upbringing.

Among Emily's biographers there are some who see Bramwell in Heathcliff (others, bearing in mind Emily's alleged lesbian tendencies, believe that Heathcliff is Emily's portrait of herself as a lonely outsider).

Bramwell himself claimed that he wrote at least a part of Wuthering Heights. A statement denied by almost everybody except Emily Brontë.

Wuthering Heights on film

1920   Bioscope
       Hindley (Warwick Ward)

1939   Goldwyn United Artists
       Hindley (Hugh Williams)

1953   *Abismos de Pasion/Les Hauts de Hurlevant*
       Mexican production, directed by Luis Bunuel

1970   American International
       Hindley (Julian Glover)

Wuthering Heights in the theatre

1933   Croydon Repertory
1939   Brixton
1940   Croydon Repertory
1943   Croydon (Grand)
1946   Granville Theatre
1947   Gateway Theatre
1947   Intimate Theatre
1948   Wimbledon Theatre
1949   People's Palace
1949   Richmond Theatre
1958   Theatre Royal, Margate
1960   Municipal Hall, Newcastle
1964   New Theatre, Bromley
1966   Victoria Theatre, Stoke
1969   Theatre Royal, Windsor
1972   Harrogate
1974   Chester Gatehouse
1974   Richmond Theatre, Yorkshire
1974   Bournemouth Playhouse

Wuthering Heights in print

(A selected list)

1847 *Wuthering Heights* by Ellis Bell (alias Emily Brontë) with *Agnes Grey* by Acton Bell (alias Anne Brontë)
Thomas Cautley Newby, Publisher (London)

1850 A new edition, revised, with a biographical notice of the authors, a selection from their literary remains, and a preface by Currer Bell (Charlotte Brontë)

1890 Cassell's Red Library (London)

1907 J. M. Dent & Co (London), E. P. Dutton & Co (New York), introduction by the editor, E. Rhys

1924 G. G. Harrap & Co (London), illustrated by Percy Tarrant

1926 Jonathan Cape (London), introduction by Rose Macaulay

1933 T. Nelson & Sons (London), illustrated by C. E. Brock

1940 Heritage Press (New York and London), Lithographs by Barnett Freedman

1946 Penguin Harmondsworth

1955 Macdonald (London), introduction by Daphne du Maurier, illustrated by W. Stein

1961 Hamilton & Co (London, Dublin)

1964 Folio Society (London), Lithographs by Charles Keeping

Hugh Williams as Hindley and Lawrence Olivier as Heathcliff in the 1939 screen version of *Wuthering Heights*.

Brian de Bois Guilbert

From **Ivanhoe** By **Sir Walter Scott**

'. . . a man past forty, thin, strong, tall and muscular; an athletic figure, which long fatigue and constant exercise seemed to have left none of the softer part of the human form, having reduced the whole to brawn, bones, and sinews, which had sustained a thousand toils, and were ready to dare a thousand more. . . . High features, naturally strong and powerfully expressive, had been burnt almost into Negro blackness by constant exposure to the tropical sun. . . . His keen, piercing, dark eyes, told in every glance a history of difficulties subdued, and danger dared, and seemed to challenge opposition to his wishes, for the pleasure of sweeping it from his road by a determined exertion of courage and of will; a deep scar on his brow gave additional sternness to his countenance, and a sinister expression to one of his eyes, which had been slightly injured on the same occasion, and of which the vision, though perfect, was in a slight and partial degree distorted. . . .'
Sir Walter Scott

The Story

Embittered after being jilted by the daughter of a penniless Baron of Bordeaux, Sir Brian de Bois Guilbert, a Norman knight, famed for his daring, joins the celibate order of the Knights Templar.

In England, returning from the Crusades, de Bois Guilbert and Reginald Front de Boeuf kidnap the rich jew, Isaac of York and his daughter Rebecca, intending to hold them for ransom. De Bois Guilbert becomes infatuated with Rebecca and tries to seduce her. She threatens to throw herself out of her prison tower when the castle is stormed by a band of outlaws led by Robin of Locksley and King Richard disguised anonymously as the Black Knight. De Bois Guilbert escapes with Rebecca to the lodge of the Knights Templar. The Templars, believing that Rebecca has bewitched De Bois Guilbert, condemn her to be burnt to death as a sorceress. She claims the right of a champion to defend her. De Bois Guilbert visits her once more to affirm his love and offer to leave the Templars for her sake, but she refuses him. Ironically chosen to represent the Templars in combat with Rebecca's champion, Ivanhoe, and his old enemy, De Bois Guilbert dies before a blow is struck, 'a victim to the violence of his own contending passions'.

The Background

During the Holy Wars communications with Europe were maintained in the Holy Land by an order of knights which originated in France. After the Christian victory, pilgrims from all over Europe made the journey to the Holy Land. Unarmed and unprotected they were easy victims for the Turks. The French knights dedicated themselves to the defence and shelter of the pilgrims and changed their order to a religious–military one. They assumed the title of Templars and became a select order, recruiting only men of noble birth who donated their wealth and estates to the order. In 1128 the Council of Troyes approved the Templars. Pope Honorius gave them a plain white mantle to symbolise their purity and Pope Eugenius a red cross for the martyrdom they must endure. They wore linen coifs and red caps close over them; shirts and stockings of twisted mail, a sopra vest and broad belts with swords inserted. All was covered by a long white cloak. Unlike other orders the Knights Templar were allowed to grow beards.

After the loss of Acre, the surviving Templars left Cyprus and settled down to a quieter life. In 1312, after a struggle for power with the Pope, King Philippe the Fair of France confiscated the wealth of the Templars and imprisoned as many of the knights as he could find. He accused them of black magic, heresy, and perversion, and forced their confessions under torture. Having secured the election of a French Pope, Phillipe persuaded him to dissolve the order of the Templars. The Grand Master, James Molai, retracted his confession and was burnt as a lapsed heretic.

George Sanders as Bois de Guilbert in the 1952 screen version of *Ivanhoe*.

Ivanhoe on film

Silent

1913   Herbert Brencon Productions

Sound

1952   MGM
Starring George Sanders
as Bois de Guilbert

1960s   Columbia TV Series
(loosely based on Scott's character in a series of weekly adventures)

1960   BBC Television Production. Screen Gems. Distributed by Columbia Pictures

Ivanhoe on the stage

1862   An extravaganza
by H. J. Byron
The Strand Theatre

1913   A Drama (from the novel)
The Lyceum Theatre

1891   An Opera
by Julian Sturgess
(from Scott's novel)
Music by Sir Arthur Sullivan
The Royal English Opera House
(later the Palace Theatre)

Ivanhoe in print

(*A selected list*)

First published in 1819

1843   Robert Cadell (Edinburgh)

1875   Geo. Routledge & Sons (London and New York), designs by George Cruikshank and others

1880   Ward Lock & Co (London), with notes by the author

1897   Service and Paton (London), illustrated by C. E. Brock

1900   Clarendon Press (Oxford), introduction and notes by C. E. Theodosius

1904   Blackie & Son (Glasgow), illustrated by A. Pearse

1906   Ginn & Co (Boston), edited by W. D. Lewis

1910   Cassell & Co (London), illustrated by G. Soper

1922   G. G. Harrap & Co. (London), illustrated by Rowland Wheelwright

1938   T. Nelson & Sons (London), with notes

1953   Collins (London), introduction by Sir H. J. C. Grierson

1958   Ginn & Co, edited by M. W. & G. Thomas, illustrated by Faith Jacques

1964   Longmans (London), appendixes and notes by A. J. Brayley

1972   Studio Vista (London), edited and abridged by Robin S. Wright, illustrated by Chris. Bradbury

Combat between Bois de Guilbert and the Disinherited
Knight. A nineteenth-century engraving after A. Marie.

Mr Grimes

From **The Water Babies** By **Charles Kingsley**

'His master was so delighted at his new customer
that he knocked Tom down out of hand, and drank
more beer that night than he usually did in two, in
order to be sure of getting up in time next morning; for the more a man's head aches when he
wakes, the more glad he is to turn out, and have a
breath of fresh air. And when he did get up at four
the next morning, he knocked Tom down again, in
order to teach him (as young gentlemen used to be
taught at public schools) that he must be an extra
good boy that day, as they were going to a very
great house, and might make a very good thing of
it, if they could but give satisfaction.'
Charles Kingsley

**An illustration of Mr Grimes by G. Soper from the
1923 edition of *The Water Babies*.**

The Story

Mr Grimes is a master sweep and part-time poacher who cruelly bullies his little apprentice, Tom. He was born and bred in Vendale, a town in the North of England, where his mother kept a school. After he left home and 'took up with the sweeps' she never heard of him again but she wept and prayed for him every night.

Tom, after being wrongfully accused of theft, runs away from Grimes and is believed drowned. Grimes, on a poaching expedition, falls into a fight and is pushed into the river. He is taken by the fairies to the Other-end-of-Nowhere where he is made to sweep the chimneys of a huge prison and to suffer in the same way that Tom suffered, until he eventually finds himself stuck fast in a chimney with only his head and shoulders showing over the top. There he stays for years. One day he is visited by Tom who was not drowned but has become a Water Baby. Tom's kindness and the memory of his neglected mother move Grimes to tears of remorse which wash away the mortar from between the bricks, setting him free, but his punishment is not complete, and he is sent to serve the rest of his time at Mount Etna, sweeping out the crater.

The Background

In England, during the eighteenth and nineteenth centuries, half-starved and half-clothed children were apprenticed to master chimney sweeps. Often, while climbing the maze of chimneys in a big house, some lost their way and others stifled to death. Many died of 'Chimney Sweep's Cancer', thought to be caused by 'the acrimonious quality of the soot, and by obstructed perspiration, in consequence of the children being too seldom washed and cleaned of the soot, and too thinly clad to resist the cold'.*

Chimney sweeping was an overcrowded trade and many master sweeps employed more apprentices than they could afford to keep. The master was likely to live in lodgings with only one room for himself, his wife and his children; and another, 'generally a cellar without a fireplace, for his soot and apprentices; without any means of providing for their health, or cleanliness.*

The boys would sleep on the soot bags used during their day's work. If the child survived his apprenticeship, his only hope, having been denied any other education or training, was to become a journeyman sweep earning £3 to £6 a year. He might eventually become a master sweep and when he joined the unequal struggle for employment, earn himself the right to subject his apprentices to the same tortures suffered by himself as a 'climbing boy'.

The Water Babies in the theatre

Garrick Theatre, London
Fairy play by Rutland Barrington (from the book by Charles Kingsley)
Music by F. Rosse, A. Fox and Alfred Cellier
Mr Grimes (Webb Darleigh)

1903 Revival at the Garrick Theatre

1973 The Royalty Theatre, London
(from the play by Charles Kingsley)
Book, music and lyrics by John Taylor
Mr Grimes (Jacob Witkin)

The Water Babies in print

(A selected list)

1863 London & Cambridge
1864 Macmillan & Co (London)
1869 London, illustrated by Sir N. Paton and P. Skelton
1886 Macmillan & Co (London), illustrated by L. Sambourne
1905 Geo. Routledge & Sons (London), illustrated by May Sandheim
1908 J. M. Dent & Co (London), E. P. Dutton & Co (New York), illustrated by Margaret W. Tarrant
1915 Constable & Co (London), illustrated by W. Heath Robinson
1923 G. Allen & Unwin (London), illustrated by G. Soper
1934 Hutchinson & Co (London), illustrated by Ena M. Rollason
1947 P. R. Gawthorn (London), illustrated by Emil Weiss
1948 Oxford University Press (London), illustrated by A. E. Jackson
1954 Hamlyn Classics (London)
1956 Juvenile Productions (London), illustrated
1964 Blackie & Son (London and Glasgow)
1966 Collins (London). Retold by Lavinia Derwent, illustrated by Dennis Carabine

The Water Babies has never been produced as a film.

---

* From a report on chimney sweeps by the Society for Bettering the Poor, 4 December 1797.

Margaret Rutherford as Mrs Danvers in the 1940 stage production of *Rebecca* at the Queen's Theatre.

Mrs Danvers

From **Rebecca** By **Daphne du Maurier**

'Someone advanced from the sea of faces, someone tall and gaunt, dressed in deep black, whose prominent cheekbones and great, hollow eyes gave her a skull's face, parchment-white, set on a skeleton's frame. She came towards me, and I held out my hand, envying her for her dignity and her composure; but when she took my hand her's was limp and heavy, deathly cold, and it lay in mine like a lifeless thing. "This is Mrs Danvers," said Maxim, and she began to speak, still leaving that dead hand in mine, her hollow eyes never leaving my eyes, so that my own wavered and would not meet hers, and as they did, so her hand moved in mine, the life returned to it, and I was aware of a sensation of discomfort and shame.'

Daphne du Maurier

Judith Anderson as Mrs Danvers and Joan Fonteyn as Mrs de Winter in the 1940 screen version of *Rebecca*.

The Story

Since Rebecca's childhood, Mrs Danvers has been her adoring personal maid and confidante. When Rebecca marries Maxim De Winter and becomes mistress of Manderlay, Mrs Danvers goes with her. Self-willed and cruel, Rebecca deliberately destroys an outwardly perfect marriage, plotting her outrageous exploits with the devoted 'Danny'.

Rebecca is drowned and Mrs Danvers is heartbroken. She remains at Manderlay as housekeeper. Rebecca's room is kept exactly as if she is still alive. When the new Mrs De Winter arrives, young and awkward, Mrs Danvers tries, in her bitterness, to break her, nearly succeeding in talking her into suicide.

It is discovered that Rebecca's drowning had not been an accident. Unknown even to Mrs Danvers, she found she was dying of cancer and appeared to have taken her own life. Shocked by the news (and perhaps guessing the truth—that Rebecca was in fact murdered by Maxim) Mrs Danvers, silently and without trace, leaves Manderlay. That night it is burnt to the ground.

Rebecca on film

1940   Selznick Production
        Distributed by United Artists
        Mrs Danvers (Judith Anderson)

Rebecca in the theatre

1940   The Queen's Theatre, London
        Play by Daphne du Maurier from her novel
        Mrs Danvers (Margaret Rutherford)

1942   The Strand Theatre, London
        Mrs Danvers (Mary Merrill)

1942   The Ambassadors Theatre, London
        Mrs Danvers (Georgina Winter)

1943   The Scala Theatre, London
        Mrs Danvers (Louise Hampton)

Rebecca in print

(*A selected list*)

1938   Victor Gollancz (London)

1940   Victor Gollancz (London) (A play in 3 Acts)

1944   French's Acting Edition (London)

1957   Longmans, Green & Co (London), illustrated by John Brinkworth, simplified and abridged by A. S. M. Ronaldson

1961   Longmans, Green & Co (London)

1962   Penguin Books (Harmondsworth)

1965   F. A. Thorpe (Ulverscroft)
        Ulverscroft Large Print Series

1971   Editor Service (Geneva) (part of a collection distributed by Heron Books), illustrated by Sandra Archibald, frontispiece by B. R. Linklater

Brer Fox

From Uncle Remus By Joel Chandler Harris

'One time Brer Rabbit and Brer Fox went out in de woods huntin', and atter so long a time, dey' gun ter git hongry. Leas'ways Brer Fox did, kaze Brer Rabbit had brung a ashcake in his wallet, en eve'y time he got a chance he'd eat a mou'ful—eve'y time Brer Fox'd turn his back, Brer Rabbit 'd nibble at it. Well, endurin' er de day, Brer Fox 'gun ter get mighty hongry. Dey had some game what they done kill, but dey wuz a fur ways fum home, en dey ain't had no fier fer ter cook it.

'Dey don't what ter do. Brer Fox so hongry it make his head ache. Bimeby de sun gun ter git low, en it shine red thoo de trees.

'Brer Rabbit: "low, Yonder, whar you kin git some fier". Brer Fox say, "Wharbouts?" Brer Rabbit: "low, Down whar de sun is. She'll go in her hold terrectly, en den you kin git a big chunk er fier. Des leave yo' game here wid me, en go git de fier. You er de biggest en de swiftest, en kin go quicker."

'Wid dat Brer Fox put out ter whar de sun is. He trot, he lope, en he gallup, en bimeby he git dar. But by dat time de sun done gone down in her hole end de groun', fer ter take a night's rest, en Brer Fox he can't git no fier. He holler en holler, but de sun ain't pay no 'tention. Den Brer Fox git mad en say he gwine ter stay der twel he git some fier. So he lay down topper de hole, en 'fo' he knowed it he drapt asleep. Dar he wuz, en dar whar he got kotch. Now you know might well de sun bleedz ter rise. Yo' pa kin tell you dat. En when she start ter rise, dar wus Brer Fox fas' asleep right 'pon topper de hole whar she got to rise fum. When dat de case, sump'n n'er bleedz ter happen. De sun rise up, an when she fin' Brer Fox in de way, she het him up an scorch his legs twel dey got right black. Dey got black, en dey black ter dis ve'y day.

' "What became of Brer Rabbit?" the little boy asked. Uncle Remus laughed, or pretended to laugh, until he bent double.

' "Shoo, honey," he exclaimed, when he could catch his breath, "time Brer Fox got out'n sight, Brer Rabbit tuck all de game en put out fer home. En dar whar you better go yo'se'f. . . ." '

Joel Chandler Harris (Why Brother Fox's legs are black)

The Story

By no means is Brother Fox the wiliest of the 'creeturs'. Although he uses all his cunning to cheat and trick the other animals, he has not yet succeeded. Brer Rabbit is chief among his adversaries, and although Brer Fox has not beaten him yet, an inferior creature—such as a rabbit—stands little chance when a superior creature—such as a fox—is really trying. Everyone knows that—don't they?

The Background

Joel Chandler Harris, employed as a journalist on the *Atlanta Constitution*, was asked to write some dialect stories in the style of a former contributor, Sam W. Small. Harris wrote a sketch involving a conversation between an old and a young negro. The old negro he called Uncle Remus. In 1876 the *Atlanta Constitution* published more of Harris's dialect sketches. Harris gradually dropped all the characters except Uncle Remus who became a straightforward teller of tales. In 1879 Harris hit upon the idea of telling the old plantation folk tales through the words of Uncle Remus, and the first Brer Rabbit, Brer Fox tale appeared on 20 July. Harris started his famous collection of folk songs and tales and they were published in book form in 1893 under the title 'Uncle Remus and his friends, Old Plantation stories, songs and ballads with sketches of Negro characters.

Uncle Remus on film

1946 Walt Disney/R.K.O.
Re-titled
The Song of the South
(Combined cartoon and live action)

Brer Fox in the 1946 Walt Disney screen version
Song of the South.

Uncle Remus in print

(A selected list)

1880 *Uncle Remus, his Songs and his Sayings.*
D. Appleton & Co., illustrated by
F. S. Church

1881 *Uncle Remus, or Mr Fox, Mr Rabbit &*
Mr Terrapin. Routledge & Sons (London)

1883 *Nights with Uncle Remus.* (Myths and legends
of the Old Plantation.) J. R. Osgood & Co.,
illustrated

1892 *Uncle Remus and his friends* (Old Plantation
Stories Songs and Ballads)

1905 *Told by Uncle Remus.* McClure Phillips & Co.,
illustrated

1906 *Uncle Remus.* Thos. Nelson & Sons (London),
illustrated by Harry Rountree and Rene Bull

1907 Alexander Moring, illustrated by
J. A. Shepherd

1909 *Uncle Remus and Brer Rabbit.* W. & R.
Chambers (Edinburgh), illustrated

1910 *Uncle Remus and the Little Boy.* Small,
Maynard & Co., illustrated by
J. M. Conde

1920 *Uncle Remus.* D. Appleton & Co.,
illustrated by A. B. Frost & E. W. Kemble)

1935 *Uncle Remus* (or the story of Mr Fox and
Mr Rabbit). T. Nelson & Sons (London)

1949 *The Essential Uncle Remus.* Jonathan Cape
(London), edited by George Van Sanlvoord &
Archibald C. Coalidge

Harry Flashman

From **Tom Brown's Schooldays** By **Thomas Hughes**

'Here come Speedicut and Flashman, the School House bully, with shouts and great action. Won't you two come up to young Brooke after locking up by the School House fire, with "Old fellow, wasn't that just a splendid scrummage by the three trees! But he knows you, and so do we. You don't really want to drive that ball through that scrummage, chancing all hurt for the glory of the School House, but to make us think that's what you want—a vastly different thing, and fellows of your kidney will never go through more than the skirts of a scrummage where it's all push and no kicking. We respect boys who keep out of it, and don't sham going in; but you—we had rather not say what we think of you!" '
Thomas Hughes

Flashman's defeat illustrated by Arthur Hughes from the 1869 edition of *Tom Brown's Schooldays*.

The Story

Archetypal, irredeemable school bully and all-round cad, Flashman, as a young schoolboy had been a first-class 'toady', and now, as a fifth former, his cruel bullying of the 'small fry' and abuse of the 'fagging' system (fags being officially reserved for sixth formers) causes a fairly successful rebellion by the younger boys, led by Tom Brown and East. After losing a fight with Tom and East, Flashman no longer attacks them physically, but does all in his power to discredit them. Deceptively well-built for his seventeen years, with an ability to appear pleasant if needed, and possessing a shrewd business sense, he manages to stay popular with some of his contemporaries. Whilst still in the fifth form he is discovered drunk in the street by a master from Rugby school and expelled. But the results of his malice against Tom Brown and East remain effective long after he has gone.

The Background

Anyone under the impression that the progress of Harry Flashman was in any way cut short when the gates of Rugby clanged shut on him, is, I am happy to say, much mistaken. Thanks to Mr George Macdonald Fraser, the glittering career of the King of the cads is now revealed in its entirety. Mr Fraser has put into book form '. . . the great mass of manuscript known as the Flashman papers . . . discovered during a sale of household furniture at Ashby, Leicestershire in 1965. . . . .' A point of major literary interest about the papers is that they clearly identify Flashman, the school bully of Thomas Hughes *Tom Brown's Schooldays*, with the celebrated Victorian soldier of the same name. The papers are in fact, Harry Flashman's memoirs from the day of his expulsion from Rugby school in the late 1830s to the early years of the present century. He appears to have written them some time between 1900 to 1905, when he must have been over eighty.

Mr Fraser has included in his book what appears to be an extract from the British publication *Who's Who*:

FLASHMAN, Harry Paget, Brigadier General, vc, KCB, KCIE, Chevalier, Legion d'honneur, US Medal of Honour; San Serafino Order of Purity and Truth, 4th Class. b. 1822, s. H. Flashman Esq, Ashby, and Hon. Alicia Paget; Educ. Rugby School; m. Elspeth Rennie Morrison, d. Lord Paisley; one d., served Afghanistan, 1841–2 (medals, thanks of Parliament), Crimea (Staff), Indian Mutiny (Lucknow, etc, VC); China, Taiping Rebellion, etc. . . .

Thomas Hughes, who wrote only of Flashman's adventures as a schoolboy, would have been greatly surprised by Mr Fraser's momentous discovery.

Tom Brown's Schooldays in the theatre

1972 A musical: 'Tom Brown's Schooldays';
Cambridge Theatre, London
Flashman (Christopher Guard)

Tom Brown's Schooldays on film

Silent

1916 The Windsor Film Company
Flashman (Jack Hobbs)

Sound

1940 Flashman (Billy Halop)
1951 Renown/George Minter
Flashman (John Forrest)

Tom Brown's Schooldays in print

(*A selected list*)

1857 Macmillan & Co (Cambridge)
1858 Bernard Tauchnitz (Liepzig)
1869 Macmillan (London), illustrated by Arthur Hughes and Sidney Prior Hall
1871 Harper & Bros (New York), illustrated by Hughes and Prior Hall
1899 Temple Classics, illustrated by T. H. Robinson
1904 Methuen & Co (London), introduction and notes by V. Rendall
1905 Harmondsworth
1907 Oxford University Press (Oxford), illustrated by H. M. Brock
1910 Cassell & Co. (London), illustrated by Gordon Browne
1911 Harper & Bros (New York & London), illustrated at Rugby School by Louis Rhead with introduction by W. D. Howells
1913 Sidgwick & Jackson (London), Preface by Lord Kilbracken, edited by F. Sidgwick
1923 G. G. Harrap & Co (London), illustrated by Percy Tarrant
1944 J. M. Dent & Sons
1951 Ward Lock & Co (London), illustrated (with narrative based on Renown Film Production)
1953 Collins (London & Glasgow), introduction by Lord Elton, illustrated by Will Nickless
1958 Macmillan & Co (London), illustrated by Edmund J. Sullivan
1969 Macmillan & Co, adapted by Marie Coghill
The Flashman Papers by George Macdonald Fraser
1969 *Flashman.* Herbert Jenkins (London)
1970 *Flashman.* (London)
Royal Flash

Polyphemus the Cyclops

From **The Odyssey** By **Homer**

'. . . When to the nearest verge of land we drew,
Fast by the sea a lonely cave we view,
High, and with darkening laurels covered o'er;
Where sheep and goats lay slumbering round the
  shore;
Near this, a fence of marble from the rock,
Brown with o'erarching pine and spreading oak,
A giant shepherd here his flock maintains
Far from the rest, and solitary reigns,
In shelter thick of horrid shade reclined;
And gloomy mischiefs harbour in his mind.
A form enormous! far unlike the race
Of human birth, in stature, or in face;
As some lone mountain's monstrous growth he
  stood,
Crowned with rough thickets, and a nodding
wood. . .'
Homer (Trans. Alexander Pope)

The Story

During their wanderings, Odysseus and his companions come to the inhospitable land of the Cyclops, the one-eyed Giants. They find the isolated cave of Polyphemus, Chief of the Cyclops, and son of the God Poseidon. They ask him for hospitality. He seizes two of the men, dashes them against the cave wall and devours their remains. Four others suffer the same fate. Trapped in the cave with him they offer the Giant wine which they have brought from the ship. When he has drunk himself insensible they gouge out his eye with a stake heated in the fire. The Cyclops keeps his sheep in the cave at night. Odysseus and his men escape by clinging to the underbellies as they are let out in the morning. Once away from the cave, Odysseus taunts his enemy from the safety of his ship. Maddened with pain, and helpless in his blindness, Polyphemus tries, unsuccessfully to sink the boat by breaking off the top of a mountain and hurling it towards the ship. He then calls to his father, Poseidon, to bring suffering to Odysseus. Poseidon hears him and Odysseus is doomed to more hardship before the end of his wanderings.

Polyphemus the Cyclops by Romano.

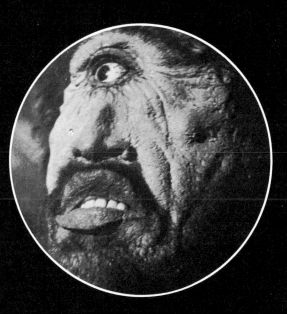

Polyphemus the Cyclops from the 1968 screen version of Ulysses.

Polyphemus the Cyclops by F. J. du Roueray—a nineteenth-century interpretation.

The Background

The Homeric Cyclops were fearsome, one-eyed, cannibalistic giants who lived in isolated caves and tended herds of sheep. They were infamous for their terrorising of strangers who landed on their shores.

The Cyclops of Greek mythology lived under Mount Etna where they served as smiths in the forges of the fire-god, Hephaestus. They forged a helmet for Hades which made the wearer invisible, a trident for Poseidon which could shake the earth and sea, and the thunderbolt of Zeus. When Zeus killed Ascelpius, the God of medicine, with his thunderbolt, Apollo, father of Ascelpius, killed in revenge the Cyclops who had fashioned the thunderbolt.

The first Cyclops to appear in Greek mythology were the sons of Uranus and Gaea: Argus—lightning, Steropes—storm clouds, Brontes—thunder.

Cyclops on film

Silent

1912   Milano Films

Sound

1965   Encyclopaedia Britannica/Rank Dramatisation

1968   Avventure de Ulisse produced by Dino de Laurentis, distributed by Paramount

The Odyssey in print

(*A selected list*)

1616   Imprinted for Nathaniel Butter, translated from the Greek by George Chapman

1665   Thomas Roycroft, translated, adorned with sculpture and illustrated with annotations by John Ogilby

1675   Printed for W. Crook, translated by Thos. Hobbes of Malmsbury (with large preface, concerning the Vertues of an Heroique Poem, written by the translator)

1725   Bernard Lintot, translated by Pope, W. Broome & E. Fenton, notes by W. Broome

1760   Printed for A. Horace, P. Virgil and T. Cicero in Paternoster Row; J. Milton in St Paul's Churchyard; and D. Plato and A. Pope in the Strand.

1753   Printed R. Urie, sold Daniel Baxter (Glasgow), translated by Alexander Pope, Esq (4 volumes)

1806   F. J. Du Raveray, translated by Pope (with plates)

1853   Ingram, Cooke & Co, translated by Pope with notes by Rev. Theodore Buckley, designed by Flaxman.

1834   G. & W. Nicol; J. Murray (London), translated by William Sotheby

1857   J. R. Smith, translated by George Chapman, introduction and notes by Richard Hooper (2 volumes)

1861   W. Blackwood & Sons (Edinburgh and London), translated in the Spenserian stanza by P. S. Worsley (2 volumes)

1869   James Parker & Co (London), translated Revd. L. Bigge Wither

1879   Macmillan & Co (London), translated S. H. Butcher and A. Long

1887   Reeves and Turner (London), translated William Morris

1900   Longmans, Green & Co (London), translated by Samuel Butler

1924   The Medici Society (London & Boston), illustrated by W. Russell Flint, translated S. H. Butcher and A. Lang

1938   T. Nelson and Sons (London), translated by W. H. D. Rouse, illustrated by Norman Hall

1945   Penguin (Harmondsworth), translated by E. V. Rieu

1965   Panther Books (London), translated by Robert Fitzgerald

Squire Thornhill

From **The Vicar of Wakefield** By **Oliver Goldsmith**

'She thought him therefore a very fine gentleman; and such as consider what powerful ingredients a good figure, fine clothes, and fortune are in that character, will easily forgive her. Mr Thornhill, notwithstanding his real ignorance talked with ease, and could expatiate upon the common topics of conversation with fluency. . . .'
Oliver Goldsmith

The Story

Sir William Thornhill, a gentleman of fortune and great virtue, allows his nephew to live as squire on his country estate. The squire is a villainous rake— a seducer of young girls, whom he takes to London, then abandons to lives of prostitution.

The Vicar of Wakefield, having fallen on hard times, takes up the modest 'cure' of the neighbourhood. Squire Thornhill entices away his daughter, Olivia, and goes through a bogus marriage ceremony with her. She escapes and is brought home by her father. In revenge the Squire attempts to ruin the family. The vicar is thrown into a debtors' prison. But the family is saved by Sir William Thornhill, who has fallen in love with, and eventually marries, the vicar's youngest daughter. The squire is unmasked, and it is discovered, that unknown to him, he and Olivia were married by a real priest. Sir William Thornhill bestows a large fortune on Olivia and banishes Squire Thornhill from his estate for ever.

The Background

In 1763 Samuel Johnson was instrumental in selling *The Vicar of Wakefield* and saving Oliver Goldsmith from eviction.

'I received one morning a message from poor Goldsmith that he was in great distress, and as it was not in his power to come to me, begging that I would come to him as soon as possible. I sent him a guinea, and promised to come to him directly. I accordingly went as soon as I was dressed, and found that his landlady had arrested him for his rent, at which he was in a very violent passion. I perceived that he had already changed my guinea, and had got a bottle of Madeira and a glass before him. I put the cork in the bottle, desired he would be calm, and began to talk to him of the means by which he might be extricated. He then told me he had a novel ready for the press, which he produced to me. I looked into it, and saw its merit told the landlady I would soon return and having gone to a bookseller, sold it for sixty pounds. I brought Goldsmith the money, and he discharged his rent, not without rating his landlady in a high tone for having used him so ill.'

COOKE'S EDITION OF SELECT BRITISH NOVELS.

VICAR OF WAKEFIELD. VOL. II. Ch. 4 P.
Olivia rejecting with disdain the offer of
a Purse of Money from Squire Thornhill.

The Vicar of Wakefield on film

There have been two silent versions

1912 Pathe/Britannia Films

1913 Planet Films

1913 Filmed and Produced by the Hepworth Manufacturing Company (Controlled by the Kinematograph Trading Company) Squire Thornhill (Harry Gilbey)

1916 Ideal Films

The Vicar of Wakefield in the theatre

1850 Strand Theatre, London
Dramatised from the book by J. S. Coyne.

1906 Prince of Wales Theatre, London
A light Opera
Lyrics by Laurence Housman
Music by Liza Lehmann

The Vicar of Wakefield in print

(*A selected list*)

1766 F. Newbery (London) (Printed by B. Collins), 2 volumes, 1st edition

1769 F. Newbery (London), 4th edition, 2 volumes

1772 William Mentz (Philadelphia), 2 volumes

1803 Louis (Paris), A new edition with notes

1798 D. Walker (Hereford), embellished with woodcuts by T. Bewick

1789 Joseph Wenman (Wenman's Cheap edition), with plates

Opposite:
An eighteenth-century engraving from *The Vicar of Wakefield*.

1780 Hanison & Co (The Novelist's Magazine), with plates

1792 F. Harding & Co., with engravings by Thos. Stothard

1818 John Sharpe, with engravings from the designs of Richard Westall

1820 Deane & Mundy (revised and corrected, with the life of the author, by Dr Samuel Johnson)

1823 Ballantyne's Novelists Library, preface by Sir Walter Scott

1832 James Cochrane & Co, edited by Thomas Roscoe, illustrated by George Cruikshank

1886 John Hogg (with biographical sketch of Goldsmith by Henry J. Nicoll), illustrated by William Mulready

1898 Service and Paton, illustrated by C. E. Brock

1900 Century Co (New York), introduction by Henry James

1904 Cassell & Co (London), introduction by Sir Henry Irving

1929 Geo. G. Harrap & Co (London), illustrated by Arthur Rackham

1938 Thomas Nelson & Sons (London), illustrated by C. E. Brock ('Life of Goldsmith' by Sir Walter Scott)

1944 Penguin (Harmondsworth)

1952 The Folio Society (London), illustrated by Margaret Wetherbee

The Vicar of Wakefield has been translated into Polyglot, French, Czech, Danish, Dutch, Estonian, Finnish, German, Greek, Hungarian, Polish, Irish, Rumanian, Russian, Serbo-Croat, Spanish, Swedish.

Rupert of Hentzau

From **The Prisoner of Zenda** and **Rupert of Hentzau** By Anthony Hope

DOUGLAS FAIRBANKS JR
S.I.P. 103 - P-75-C

'Young Rupert, who looked like a daredevil, and could not have been more than twenty-two or twenty-three, took the lead . . . splendidly horsed and superbly equipped . . . with an insolent smile on his curling lip and a toss of his thick hair—he was a handsome villain, and the gossip ran that many a lady had troubled her heart for him already.

'For my part, if a man must be a knave, I would have him a debonair knave, and I liked Rupert Hentzau better than his long-faced, close-eyed companions.

'It makes your sin no worse, as I conceive it, to do it à la mode and stylishly.

'. . . young Rupert went about Satan's work with a smile in his eye and a song on his lip. . . .'
Anthony Hope

The Story

Rupert of Hentzau, handsome and dashing, is a member of the 'Group of Six', led by Prince Michael of Streslau, who intends to usurp the throne of the newly proclaimed King, his ineffectual brother, Rudolf V. On the eve of the coronation they drug Rudolf, hoping to present Michael in his stead at the ceremony. But the King's place is taken at the ceremony by an Englishman, Rudolf Rassendyl, who is visiting the country. He is the descendant of a bastard sired by Rudolf II, the King's ancestor, and bears a strong family resemblance. At the coronation he meets and falls in love with Flavia who is betrothed to the King.

The 'Group of Six' capture the King and hold him prisoner in their castle at Zenda. Rupert kills Michael in a quarrel over his mistress, Madame Antoinette de Mauban. When Rassendyl rescues the King from Zenda, Rupert suggests they collaborate in murdering the King and sharing the ruling power of Ruritania. Rassendyll refuses, and there is a fight. Rupert flees to the forest and Rassendyll returns to England.

Douglas Fairbanks Jnr. as Rupert of Hentzau in the 1937 screen version of *The Prisoner of Zenda*.

Three years later Flavia is unhappily married to the King. Rupert, still a fugitive, hears that she and Rassendyll exchange red roses as love tokens every year. This year Flavia has also sent a letter. Rupert intercepts the letter, and takes it to the King at his hunting lodge in Zenda. He is attacked by the King's dog, which he kills. The King reaches for his gun in retaliation and Rupert shoots him dead, then makes his escape.

When the King's murder is discovered the lodge is burnt to the ground and Rassendyll is asked to impersonate him. He is undecided, but in the meantime he tracks down Rupert to a house in Streslau. There is a fight and Rupert is killed.

Rassendyll is also killed shortly afterwards, and buried as the King of Ruritania.

The Background

Ruritania is a kingdom in central Europe and has become very familiar in the English language. It did not exist at all until Anthony Hope invented it. The Ruritanian setting has been used by many other authors since it appeared as the setting for *The Prisoner of Zenda* in 1894.

Anthony Hope (Sir Anthony Hope Hawkins, knighted for his services to the Ministry of Information 1914–18) was born on 9 February 1863 in London. A brilliant scholar and all-round sportsman, he won a first at Balliol College, Oxford, where he became President of the Union. He found himself in a position to choose a career in politics, Law or literature. He chose law, but wrote novels in his spare time. He had written five novels—none of them successful—before he conceived the idea for *The Prisoner of Zenda*. In 1893, on 28 November, walking home after concluding a successful case, his imagination began to go to work on a new setting for a 'romantic' story. A story set in an entirely original country. As he continued to walk, two men passed him and he was struck with the similarity of their appearance. An idea for a tale of mistaken identity pushed its way into the newly formed kingdom, which, he decided, would be called Ruritania. He began to write that evening and by the end of the year *The Prisoner of Zenda* was complete. It was an immediate success and the much-looked-forward-to sequel *Rupert of Hentzau* followed in 1898.

Prisoner of Zenda on film

1915 London Film Company
Rupert (Gerald Ames)

1922 MGM
Rupert (Raymond Navarro)

1937 Selznick
Rupert (Douglas Fairbanks jnr)

1952 MGM
Rupert (James Mason)

Rupert of Hentzau

1915 London Film Company
Rupert (Gerald Ames)

1923 MGM Rupert (Lew Cody)

Prisoner of Zenda in the theatre

1896 St James Theatre
adapted by Edward Rose and revived at the Haymarket 1923

1900 St James Theatre
Rupert of Hentzau
play by Anthony Hope

Prisoner of Zenda in print

(A selected list)

1894 J. W. Arrowsmith (Bristol), 'Being the history of three months in the life of an English gentleman'

1898 J. W. Arrowsmith (Bristol) ('Being a sequel to a story entitled "The Prisoner of Zenda"'), illustrated by C. D. Gibson

1898 G. N. Morang (Toronto)

1898 J. W. Arrowsmith (Bristol), New Edition with illustrations by C. D. Gibson

1907 J. W. Arrowsmith (Bristol), illustrated by Charles Dana Gibson

1907 T. Nelson & Sons (London)

1907 T. Nelson & Sons (London) (Nelson's Library)

1918 T. Nelson & Sons (London) (Nelson's Library)

1923 J. W. Arrowsmith

1923 T. Nelson & Sons (London)

1939 Longmans Simplified English Series (London), (simplified by George F. Wear)

1940 Longman's Simplified English Series, simplified by George F. Wear, illustrated by John Nicholson

1956 *Die Gevangene Van Zenda* (Pretoria) (Vertaling Van Jacques Van Zijl), Libri-Reeks Van Klassieke Jeuglektuur

1959 *Umbanjwa wase Zenda* (Johannesburg), Iququlwe Nguguybon B. Sinxo. Xosa

1961 The Folio Society (London), illustrated by Biro

1961 Blackie & Co (London and Glasgow), 'Chosen Books', illustrated by Victor Ambrus

1962 Dent/Dutton Children's Illustrated Classics (London & New York), illustrated by Michael Godfrey

1963 Dent/Dutton (London and New York), Children's Illustrated Classics, plates and line drawings by Michael Godfrey

1966 *Prisoner of Zenda/Rupert of Hentzau*, Dent/Dutton (London and New York) (Everyman's Library) (in one volume)

The Sheriff of Nottingham

From **The Legend of Robin Hood (Folklore)**

'Robin bent a good bow,
An arrow he drew at his will,
He hit so the proud Sheriff,
Upon the ground he lay full still;
And or he might up arise,
On his feet to stand;
He smote off the Sheriff's head,
With his bright brand.
"Lie thou there, thou proud Sheriff;
Evil might thou thrive,
There might no man to thee trust
The whiles thou wert alive!" '
(*The death of the Sheriff of Nottingham, taken from
the earliest known printed tale of 'Robin Hood': 'The
Lytell geste of Robyn Hode'*)

The Story

The Sheriff of Nottingham, greedy, scheming right-
hand man to King Edward, is willing to stoop to
any deceit in order to capture the outlaws of
Sherwood Forest, Robin Hood and his men.

Captured by outlaws, he is set free on condition
that he ceases to persecute them. Robin vows to kill
him if he breaks his word. But the promise is soon
broken when the Sheriff tricks the outlaws into
leaving the forest to enter an archery contest in
Nottingham. They are set upon by the Sheriff's
men but escape and seek refuge in the house of Sir
Richard at the Lee. On hearing that Sir Richard has
helped Robin to escape, the Sheriff arrests him, at
the same time promising the King that Robin Hood
will soon be his prisoner. Hearing of Sir Richard's
arrest the outlaws rush to his rescue. In the ensuing
fight Robin kills the treacherous Sheriff with an
arrow and cuts off his head with a blow of his
sword.

The Background

Until 1448 Nottingham was run by two bailiffs
answerable to the Sheriff of Nottingham and
Derbyshire, whose jurisdiction included Sherwood
Forest. These Sheriffs can be traced back to the
Norman conquest. They were usually men of high
rank and held the most important posts in the dis-
trict, being answerable only to the King. Such
power led inevitably to corruption in some cases.
Phillip Mark, Sheriff from 1209 to 1223, is recorded
as running an extremely successful protection racket

which brought him a yearly income of 100 shillings.

'. . . for having his good will and for maintaining
the liberties of the said Burgess, and that he should
not enter those liberties. . . .'

This lucrative side line was passed on to his
successors until a court of law stopped it in 1265.
The growing importance of Justices of the Peace
from the end of the twelfth century began to limit
the power of the Sheriffs. In 1448 King Henry VI
abolished the office of Sheriff of Nottingham and
Derbyshire.

'. . . the Mayor and Burgesses shall choose in the
stead of the two Bailiffs . . . two Burgesses as
Sheriffs.' Former subservience of the Bailiffs to the
Mayor was substituted by the Sheriffs subservience
to the King only.

A few names have survived of the earliest Sheriffs:

William Malet	1068
Hugh of Baldric	?
Ranulf Fitz Ingelram	1155
Philip Mark	1209
Simon de Headon	?
Sir Walter de Eastwood	1255
Roger Michell	1356

The first consistent records of the Bailiffs were
started by the Borough of Nottingham in 1400 with
Robert de Sutton and Richard de Lyndeley. The
first Sheriffs recorded after the new charter of 1448
were John Sawyer and Thomas Ivynet. But it is
probable that the previous Bailiffs, Thomas Heth
and Thomas Mylys, were elected the first Sheriffs
of Nottingham, on 15 September 1448.

Robin Hood on film

Silents

1908	Clarendon Film Company	*Robin Hood and His Merry Men*
1910	Kalem Production Company	*Robin Hood*
1912	Etienne Arnaud Production Company	*Robin Hood*
1912		*Robin Hood Outlawed*
1913	American Standard Co	*Robin Hood*
1913	Kinemacolor Production Company	*Robin Hood*
1914	Tannhauser Productions	*Robin Hood and Maid Marion*

1922 United Artists/Fairbanks
Robin Hood
Robin Hood (Douglas Fairbanks)
The Sheriff (William Lowery)

1923 Export and Import Film Co
Robin Hood Junior
Children's version of the 1922 film dedicated
to Douglas Fairbanks
The Sheriff (Philip Dunham)

Sound

1938 Warner Bros
The Adventures of Robin Hood
Robin Hood (Erroll Flynn)
Sheriff (Melville Cooper)

1945 *Bandit of Sherwood Forest*
Robin Hood (Cornel Wilde)

1950 *Rogues of Sherwood Forest*
Robin Hood (John Derek)

1952 Walt Disney Productions
Story of Robin Hood
Robin Hood (Richard Todd)

1954 Hammer Films
Men of Sherwood Forest

1964 Warner Bros/Pathe
Robin and the Seven Hoods
Robin Hood (Frank Sinatra)
Sheriff (Victor Buono)
(Musical set in gangland Chicago in the
'twenties)

1967 Hammer Films
The Challenge of Robin Hood

Cartoons

1939 Warner Bros
Merry Melody
Popeye
Tom and Jerry

1957 Woody Woodpecker

1958 Duffy Duck
Mr Magoo

1973 Walt Disney Productions
Full-length feature cartoon
The Sheriff as a Wolf

Robin Hood in print

1506 *Here Begynneth a Lytell Geste of Robin Hode*

1514 *Robert Copland*

1601 *The Downfall of Robert, Earl of Huntingdon*,
by A. Munday and H. Chettle

1777 *The Adventures of Robert, Earl of Huntingdon*

1800 *The History and Real Adventures of Robin
Hood and His Merry Companions* by Captain
Charles Johnson

1820 *Robin Hood*; a collection of ancient poems,
songs and ballads by J. Ritson

1870 *The Story of Robin Hood* by W. Heaton

1903 *The Ballad of Robin Hood* by Edward Arber

1905 *Stories of Robin Hood and His Merry Outlaws*,
retold from the old ballads by J. W.
McSpadden

**Melville Cooper as the Sheriff of Nottingham with
Basil Rathbone and Claude Raines in the 1938 screen
version of *The Adventures of Robin Hood*.**

1908 *Robin Hood* (old ballads chosen by A. T. Quiller-Couch), Clarendon Press (Oxford)

1911 *The Ballad of Robin Hood* (from the original version) De La Mare Press (London)

1925 *The Greenwood* by Sir Henry J. Newbolt

1925 *Life and Adventures of Robin Hood* by Rowland Walker (London)

1931 *Robin Hood and Other Tales of Old England* by R. W. Hobhouse (London)

1939 *Robin Hood and his Merry Men* (The Merlin Series), by Charles Herbert (London)

1942 *The Outlaw of Sherwood Forest* by K. Smith (London)

1947 *The Adventures of Robin Hood*, Collins (London and Glasgow)

1956 *The Truth About Robin Hood* by Percy V. Harris

1958 *A Guide to the Robin Hood Country*

Robin Hood in the theatre

1906 The Lyric Theatre
A romantic play by Henry Hamilton and William Devereux

1907 Repeat at The Lyric Theatre

1931 The 'Q' Theatre

Simon Legree

From **Uncle Tom's Cabin** By **Harriet Beecher Stowe**

Theodore Roberts as Simon Legree in William A. Brady's 1901 production of *Uncle Tom's Cabin*.

'A short, broad, muscular man, in a checked shirt considerably open at the bosom, and pantaloons much the worse for dirt and wear, elbowed his way through the crowd, like one who is going actively into business. From the moment that Tom saw him approaching, he felt an immediate and revolting horror at him, that increased as he came near. He was evidently, though short, of gigantic strength. His round, bullet head, large, light-grey eyes, with their shaggy sandy eyebrows, and stiff, wiry, sun-burned hair, were rather unprepossessing items, it is to be confessed; his large, coarse mouth was distended with tobacco, the juice of which, from time to time, he ejected from him with great decision and explosive force; his hands were immensely large, hairy, sun-burned, freckled and very dirty, and garnished with long nails in a very foul condition.'
Harriet Beecher Stowe

The Story

In a Southern state of America Simon Legree was born, with the cruel, tyrannical nature of his father and a savage contempt for his gentle mother. As soon as possible he ran away to sea, after which his only meeting with his mother before she died, re-sulted in his brutal rejection of her. He became a slave trader and treated his slaves with great cruelty. One of his 'purchases' is Uncle Tom, a middle-aged Negro, faithful and trustworthy. Strengthened by his religious faith, Tom is able to accept Legree's savage treatment of him with a meekness that stirs Legree's buried conscience, causing him to hate Uncle Tom, and in the end, to have him beaten to death.

As part of a successful plot to escape, one of the slaves, playing on Legree's ignorance and super-stition, stages a realistic 'haunting'. This, combined with a conscience troubled by memories of his dying mother, turns Legree to drink and delirium tre-mens, from which he eventually dies.

The Background

In the early 1850s Harriet Beecher Stowe received a letter from her sister-in-law in which was written; 'Now, Hattie, if I could use the pen as you can, I would write something that would make this whole nation feel what an accursed thing slavery is'. And on 5 June 1851, in *The National Era*, the Washington anti-slavery weekly, the first episode of *Uncle Tom's Cabin* was published. The moving original subtitle, 'The Man that was a thing' was changed before the appearance of the first episode to the more Victorian 'Life among the lowly'. Originally intended to run for three months it was not, in fact, finished until 1 April 1852. It was first published in book form that same year. Mrs Stowe's powerful book has been acknowledged as one of the direct causes of the abolition of slavery in America, and eighty years later, the Nazis in Germany considered *Uncle Tom's Cabin* still in-fluential enough to be banned.

Uncle Tom's Cabin on film

1903	Edison
1910	Vitagraph
1918	Paramount
1919	Keystone (burlesque version)
1927	Universal

Uncle Tom's Cabin in the theatre

1852   Purdey's National Theatre, New York
Play by C. W. Taylor

1853   Purdy's National Theatre, New York
Play by G. L. Aitken

1932   *Tom*
A Ballet

1962   *La Capanna dello Zio Tom*
An Opera

Tent shows of *Uncle Tom's Cabin* were toured continuously for many years. The actors played in no other shows and were known as 'Tommers'.

Uncle Tom's Cabin in print

(*A selected list*)

1852   John P. Jewett (Boston), 2 volumes
Jewett, Proctor and Worthington, Cleveland, Ohio

1852   T. Bosworth (London), preface by the Author

1852   J. Cassell (London), illustrated by George Cruikshank

1857   George Routledge & Sons (London), preface by the Earl of Carlisle

1877   London (with a sketch of the life of J. Henson, generally known as Uncle Tom), illustrated

1882   Houghton, Mifflin & Co (Boston, Massachusetts), illustrated, with a bibliography by G. Bullen

1896   Cassell & Co (London), illustrated by J. N. Stoopendaal

1904   Adam & Charles Black (London), illustrated in colour by S. H. Vedder

1910   Cassell & Co (London), illustrated by George Soper

1923   Thomas Nelson & Sons (London) (Nelson's Standard Book for Boys and Girls), illustrated

1936   Oxford University Press (London)

1962   Belknap Press of Harvard University (Cambridge, Massachusetts), edited by Kenneth S. Lynn

1969   Chas. E. Morrill Publishing Co. (Columbus, Ohio), facsimile of the Boston edition of 1852, introduction by Howard M. Jones

Uncle Tom's Cabin has also been published in the following languages:

Afrikaans, Armenian, Czech, Danish, Dutch, Finnish, French, German, Greek, Hungarian, Italian, Portuguese, Rumanian, Russian, Serbo-Croatian, Slovene, Spanish, Swedish.

A scene from the 1852 stage production of *Uncle Tom's Cabin* at the Olympic Theatre.

Sir Percival Glyde

From **The Woman in White** By **Wilkie Collins**

'He was neither tall—nor short—he was a little below middle size. A light, active, high-spirited man—about five and forty years old, to look at. He had a pale face, and was bald over the forehead, but had dark hair over the rest of his head. His beard was shaven on his chin, but was let to grow, of a fine rich brown, on his cheeks and his upper lip. His eyes were brown too, and very bright; his nose straight and handsome and delicate enough to have done for a woman's. His hands the same. He was troubled from time to time with a dry hacking cough; and when he put up his white right hand to his mouth, he showed the red scar of an old wound across the back of it.'
Wilkie Collins

The Story

After marrying the heiress, Laura Fairlie, Sir Percival Glyde conspires with his friend Count Foscoe to 'kill' her and seize her fortune. They exchange Laura for her double, Ann Catherick, the inmate of a lunatic asylum. Ann dies of a heart attack and is buried as Lady Glyde. Laura is rescued and the plot uncovered by Walter Hartwright, Laura's former lover, and Marion Halcombe, her half-sister. Sir Percival is revealed as illegitimate, with no claim to the title he professes. With the help of Ann Catherick's mother, who has married the vestry clerk, he had altered the parish register to prove his birthright.

Mr Catherick, discovering his wife's clandestine meetings with Sir Percival, wrongly assumed that he was the father of Ann and left his wife. Sir Percival now buys her silence with a yearly income. Fearing that Ann also knows his secret, he has her committed to an asylum. Realising that his long-kept secret is about to be revealed, he returns to destroy the parish registers. But after he has locked himself in the vestry a fire breaks out. Unable to escape, he is burnt to death.

The Background

There are two villains and two heroines in *The Woman in White*—Sir Percival Glyde and Count

Foscoe, and Laura Fairlie and Marion Halcombe. Sir Percival and Laura Fairlie are as conventional a villain and a heroine as their sinning and sinned-against counterparts are unconventional. While Sir Percival's villainy is plain for all to see, the Count is never at any time suspected of intrigue. (How often in Victorian novels does one encounter a 'roly poly' villain who is kind to animals?)

If the reader of the *The Woman in White* sees the fragile romantic and colourless Laura Fairlie as the heroine, then the cruel, bullying Sir Percival is an apt villain. But if, however, the subtler shades of Wilkie Collins' novel are seen and accepted, Marion Halcombe and Count Foscoe are extraordinary and classic opponents.

The Woman in White on film

1912	Tannhauser Productions
1913	Gem Productions
1918	Tannhauser Productions
1929	Herbert Wilcox Production Sir Percival Glyde (Cecil Humphreys)
1948	Warner Bros

The Woman in White in the theatre

In 1871 the play was published by the Author as a Drama in a Prologue and Four Acts.
'Altered from the novel for performance on the stage by Wilkie Collins'
The play first produced at the Olympic Theatre on 9 October 1871

The Woman in White in print

(A selected list)

First serialised in the magazine 'conducted' by Charles Dickens, *All the Year Round* from 26 November 1859. This issue also contained the last episode of *A Tale of Two Cities*

1860	Harper & Bros (New York), illustrated
1860	Sampson Low, Son & Co (London), 3 volumes
1890	Chatto & Windus (London), illustrated by Sir John Gilbert and F. A. Fraser
1904	John Long (London), illustrated by A. T. Smith
1908	Cassell & Co (London)
1910	J. M. Dent & Sons (London), E. P. Dutton & Co (New York), introduction by Ernest Rhys
1910	Nelson's Classics (London)
1921	Oxford University Press (Oxford)
1931	Blackie & Son (London & Glasgow)
1937	Oxford University Press, abridged and simplified by L. R. H. Chapman, illustrated by Lorna R. Steele
1956	The Folio Society (London), Lithographs by Lyton Lamb
1969	Heron Books (London), introduction by E. C. R. Lorac

A still from the 1929 screen version of *The Woman in White*.

Sweeney Todd

From **The String of Pearls** By **Thomas Preskett Prest**

'The barber himself was a long, low-jointed, ill-put-together sort of fellow, with an immense mouth and such huge hands and feet that he was, in his way, quite a natural curiosity; and what was more wonderful, considering his trade there never was such a head of hair as Sweeney Todd's. We know not what to compare it to; probably it came nearest to what one might suppose to be the appearance of a thickset hedge, in which a quantity of small wire had got entangled. In truth it was a most terrific head of hair, and as Sweeney Todd kept all his combs in it—some people said his scissors likewise —when he put his head out of the shop door to see what sort of weather it was, he might have been mistaken for some Indian warrior with a very remarkable head-dress. He had a short, disagreeable kind of unmirthful laugh, which came in at all sorts of odd times when nobody else saw anything to laugh at at all, and which made some people start again, especially when they were being shaved, and Sweeney Todd would stop short in that operation to indulge in one of those cachinatory effusions. It was evident that the remembrance of some very strange and out-of-the-way joke must occasionally flit across him, and then he gave his hyena-like laugh, but it was so short, so sudden, striking upon the ear for a moment, and then gone, that people have been known to look up to the ceiling, and on to the floor all round them to know from where it had come, scarcely supposing it possible that it proceeded from mortal lips. Mr Todd squinted a little to add to his charms.'

Thomas Preskett Prest

A drawing from the acting edition of Sweeney Todd, published by Dicks Standard Plays.

The Story

Sweeney Todd, The Demon Barber of Fleet Street, kept a barber's shop next to the pie shop run by Mrs Lovett, his accomplice, whom he eventually murders. Any rich man unfortunate enough to give Todd his custom, was disposed of by means of his barber's chair, which tipped back and deposited the victim through a trap door into the vaults beneath. After Sweeney Todd had seen to it that they were well and truly 'polished off' he removed any money or jewels they had about them, cut up the bodies, and presented the remains of his victims to Mrs Lovett as filling for her famous and delicious pies. After eight years in this grisly trade Sweeney Todd was eventually caught and hanged.

The Background

The String of Pearls was first published as a serial in 'The People's Periodical and Family Library' between November 1846 and March 1847. It was issued again in 1850 in 92 penny numbers with the sub-title, 'Or, the Sailor's Gift'. The 92nd number included the new sub-title 'Or the Barber of Fleet Street'. It was not until the story was re-issued in 1876 in 48 penny issues that Sweeney Todd achieved star billing, and the story became Sweeney Todd, or the Demon Barber of Fleet Street. First produced as a play at the Britannia Theatre in Hoxton, in 1847, the seal was set on its popularity as a melodrama with Tod Slaughter's production in the late 1920s.

Sweeney Todd on film

1928   British Production
Sweeney Todd (Moore Marriott)
(Young man reading newspaper account of Sweeney Todd falls asleep in a chair and dreams that he is back in time as the character)

1936   MGM
Demon Barber of Fleet Street
Sweeney Todd (Tod Slaughter)

Sweeney Todd in the theatre

1847   The Britannia Theatre
Sweeney Todd, or the fiend of Fleet Street
by George Dibdin Pitt
Sweeney Todd (Mark Howard)

1862   The Bower Saloon
Sweeney Todd, the Barber of Fleet Street or *String of Pearls*
Drama by Frederick Hazleton

1927   New Theatre
Then and now matinee
Version by Andrew Melville
subsequently at the Kingsway Theatre in 1932

1928   The Elephant and Castle Theatre
Sweeney Todd
by Matt Wilkinson
Sweeney Todd (Tod Slaughter)

Sweeney Todd in print

The String of Pearls, or the Barber of Fleet Street
by Thomas Preskett Prest (begun by Geo. Macfanen)

Publishing history

1850   Serialised in the *People's Periodical*,
publisher E. Lloyd (London), (published in 92 parts)

THE MURDER OF THE USURER.

Two original illustrations of Sweeney Todd from the 1850 edition of *The String of Pearls*.

TODD ALARMED AT STRANGE SOUNDS WHILST PACKING HIS PLUNDER.

Svengali

From **Trilby** By **George Du Maurier**

'A tall bony individual of any age between thirty
and forty-five, of Jewish aspect, well featured but
sinister. He was very shabby and dirty, and wore a
red beret and a large velveteen cloak, with a big
metal clasp at the collar. His thick, heavy, languid,
lustreless black hair fell down behind his ears on to
his shoulders, in that musician-like way that is so
offensive to the normal Englishman. He had bold,
brilliant black eyes, with long heavy lids, a thin
sallow face, and a beard of burnt-up black, which
grew almost from his under eyelids; and over it his
moustache, a shade lighter, fell in two long spiral
twists. He went by the name of Svengali, and spoke
fluent French with a German accent and humorous
German twists and idioms, and his voice was very
thin and mean and harsh, and often broke into a
disagreeable falsetto. . . .'
George Du Maurier

The Story

In the Latin quarter of Paris, Svengali, whose sinister appearance is made tolerable only by his talent for music befriends Trilby O'Ferrall, a homeless artist's model. He uses his mesmeric powers to turn her, once tone deaf, into a world renowned singer. She can only sing when she is mesmerised, and afterwards knows nothing of what has happened to her. One night, during a concert at Drury Lane, Svengali dies of a heart attack and a bewildered Trilby 'wakes up' to find herself alone on a vast stage, facing a packed audience, and with no idea how she came to be there. Her life with Svengali has worn her out, and she dies soon afterwards. On her deathbed a photograph of Svengali is mysteriously delivered to her. As she looks at it she begins to sing again for the last time and she dies calling Svengali's name.

The Background

In January 1894, Trilby was published as a serial in the magazine *Harper's Monthly*. Many of the characters were based on Du Maurier's friends. In the March edition, 'Joe Sibley' appeared, an unmistakable portrait of James McNeill Whistler. Whistler took immediate offence and tried to sue for libel. The row dragged on and was finally settled by a public apology from *Harper's Monthly*, with undertakings to withdraw any future editions of the March number and to rewrite the 'offensive' character when Trilby appeared in book form. The success of the book in the USA amounted to mania. Every store stocked some article named after Trilby—and there were even 'Trilby' parties. In 1895 Paul Potter's dramatised version was produced at Manchester with Beerbohm Tree starring as Svengali, and Dorothea Baird playing the part of 'Trilby'. Its great success was repeated at the Haymarket Theatre in London, and later in America and Australia. A silent film appeared in 1922, and later John Barrymore starred in the first talking version entitled 'Svengali'.

Herbert Beerbohm-Tree as Svengali in the 1895 stage production of *Trilby* at the Haymarket Theatre.

Trilby (Svengali) on film

1912 The Standard Feature Film Co and the Kinematograph Co
Trilby

1914 The London Film Company
Trilby

1914 Phoenix Production Co
(A burlesque version by Pimple & Co, who specialised in parodies)
Trilby and Co

1917 The World Film Corporation Production
Directed by Maurice Tournier
Trilby

1925 First National/Richard Tully Production
Tense Moments with Authors Series
Svengali (Edmund Carew)

1931 Warner Bros
Svengali
Svengali (John Barrymore)

1954 MGM/Rank/Geo. Minter/Renown
Svengali
Svengali (Donald Wolfit)

Trilby in the theatre

Trilby by Paul Potter from the book by George du Maurier, opened at the Haymarket Theatre October 1895 with Sir Herbert Beerbohm-Tree as Svengali

Trilby in print

(A selected list)

First published as a serial in *Harper's Monthly* in January 1894

1894 Osgood, McIlvane & Co
(3 volumes)

1895 Osgood, McIlvane & Co
illustrated by the author

1931 J. M. Dent & Sons (London), E. P. Dutton & Co (New York), illustrated by the author

1947 Pan Books (London)

1947 The Folio Society (London), illustrated with pencil studies by the author

1953 Collins (London & Glasgow), introduction by James Laver

1954 Murray's Abbey Classics (London & Dublin) (abridged)

Two illustrations of Svengali by the author from the 1895 edition of the book.

Uriah Heep

From **David Copperfield** By **Charles Dickens**

'. . . I saw a cadaverous face appear at a small window on the ground floor . . . and quickly disappear. The low-arched door then opened, and the face came out. It was quite as cadaverous as it had looked in the window, though in the grain of it there was that tinge of red which is sometimes to be observed in the skins of red-haired people. It belonged to a red-haired person—a youth of fifteen, as I take it now, but looking much older—whose hair was cropped as close as the closest stubble; who had hardly any eyebrows, and no eyelashes, and eyes of a red-brown, so unsheltered and unshaded, that I remember wondering how he went to sleep. He was high shouldered and bony; dressed in decent black, with a white wisp of neckcloth; buttoned up to the throat; and had a long, lank, skeleton hand, which particularly attracted my attention. . . .

'. . . as I watched him reading . . . and following up the lines with his forefinger, I observed that his nostrils which were thin, and pointed, with sharp dints in them, had a singular and most uncomfortable way of expanding and contracting themselves, that they seemed to twinkle instead of his eyes, which hardly ever twinkled at all. . . . he had a way of writhing when he wanted to express enthusiasm, which diverted my attention from the compliment he had paid my relation, to the snaky twisting of his throat and body. . . .'
Charles Dickens

Roland Young as Uriah Heep in the 1935 screen version of *David Copperfield*.

The Story

After the death of his father, a sexton, eleven-year-old Uriah Heep was given his articles by the solicitor Mr Wickfield. Articles which he and his mother could not otherwise have afforded. Uriah constantly protests the humbleness of himself, of his station in life, his gratitude to Mr Wickfield, the impossibility of his ever aspiring to a partnership with him, and his admiration of Wickfield's daughter, Agnes. The business begins to deteriorate and Wickfield himself seems in danger of sinking with it. In spite of his 'umble status Uriah Keep is gradually seen to be taking control, and eventually becomes bold enough to make a bid for Agnes's hand in marriage —which she rejects. Through David Copperfield, Uriah has met the ebullient Mr Micawber and engages him as a clerk. Micawber exposes Uriah as an embezzler and the cause of Mr Wickfields near ruin. Uriah is sent to prison and finds that, being isolated from the outside world which led him astray, it is the ideal place for 'umble repentance— a fact which he does not cease to communicate to all around him.

The Background

David Copperfield could well be renamed Charles Dickens. He called on the experiences of his own life more than in any other of his books. His work in the blacking factory as a child (the bottle washing), his father sentenced to the debtors prison (Mr Micawber), his first job as a solicitor's clerk (Wickfields), the woman who hated donkeys and lived in a little house facing the sea (Betsy Trotwood), his lost love Maria (Dora), later in life he met Maria again. She had become fat and garrulous!

It has been observed that David Copperfield's initials are those of Charles Dickens backwards. Dickens never admitted this to be intentional, but he did admit that David Copperfield was the favourite of his books.

'. . . like many fond parents, I have in my heart of hearts a favourite child. And his name is David Copperfield.'

The imprisonment of Uriah Heep by H. K. Browne (Phiz) from the 1850 edition of the book.

Uriah Heep drawn by H. K. Browne (Phiz).

David Copperfield in the theatre

1892 Garrick Theatre
David
by Louis N. Parker and Murray Carson

1914 Her Majesty's Theatre
Dramatised by Louis N. Parker
Uriah Heep (Charles Quartermaine)

David Copperfield in print

First published in monthly parts between May 1849 to November 1850.

1850 Bradbury and Evans (London), illustrated H. K. Browne (Phiz)

1858 Bradbury and Evans (London), frontispiece by (Phiz)

1866 Chapman and Hall (London), 2 volumes

1891 Chapman and Hall (London), 2 volumes, illustrated

1900 Gresham Publishing Co (London), introduction by William Keith Leask, illustrated by William Rainey

1903 Adam and Charles Black (London), school edition, introduction and notes by A. A. Barter

1907 J. M. Dent & Co (London), E. P. Dutton & Co (New York), introduction by G. K. Chesterton

1910 Ginn and Co (Boston), edited with an introduction and notes by Philo Melvyn Buck

1910 Chapman and Hall (London), with plates

1911 Hodder and Stoughton (London), illustrated by Frank Reynolds

1911 Chapman and Hall (London), Henry Frowde (New York), illustrated by H. K. Browne (Phiz)

1912 Thos. Nelson and Sons (London)

1921 Geo. G. Harrap & Co (London), illustrated by Gertrude Demaine Hammond

1922 Cedric Chivers (Bath), with critical appreciations old and new

1925 Collins (London & Glasgow), illustrated by W. H. C. Groome

1935 Queensway Press, illustrated from the film produced by George Cukor and distributed by MGM

1962 Macmillan (New York and London), illustrations by N. M. Bodecker (afterwards Clifton Fadiman)

1966 Penguin (Harmondsworth)

1967 Pan Books (London), illustrated by Phiz

David Copperfield has been translated into Armenian, Chinese, Danish, Dutch, Estonian, Finnish, French, German, Irish, Italian, Norwegian, Rumanian, Russian, Serbo-Croat, Spanish, Swedish, Yiddish.

David Copperfield on film

Silent

1910 Edison
Love and the Law

1911 Thanhouser Production Co

1913 Cecil Hepworth Productions
Uriah Heep (Jack Hulcup)

Sound

1935 George Cukor Production
Distributed by MGM
Uriah Heep (Roland Young)
Mr Micawber (W. C. Fields)

1970 Omnibus Production Co/20th Century Fox
Uriah Heep (Ron Moody)

A drawing of Uriah Heep by Fred Barnard.

Acknowledgements

Author's acknowledgements
My thanks to: The British Film
Institute, The British Theatre
Museum at the Victoria and Albert
Museum, The American Library at
the University of London, The
Photographic Department of the
University of London, The Mansell
Collection, Messrs. Mander and
Mitchenson, The Dickens Fellowship,
The Dracula Society, The Sherlock
Holmes Society, Miss Mary Kelly of
King Features Syndicate Inc.
And particular thanks to Kenneth Pate
and Julia and Derek Parker for their
help and encouragement.

**The publishers wish to
acknowledge the following for
permission to reproduce extracts:**
The Estate of H. C. McNeile, Messrs.
Hodder & Stoughton Ltd. for
permission to quote from *Bulldog
Drummond* on page 56. Messrs. Barrie
& Jenkins (London), New American
Library Inc. (New York), Messrs.
Alfred A. Knopf (New York) for
permission to quote from *The
Flashman Papers* on page 58. The
Estate of Sax Rohmer for permission
to quote from *The Mystery of Fu
Manchu* on page 52. Macmillan
Publishing Co. Inc. (New York), The
Estate of Ian Fleming, Messrs.
Jonathan Cape, Glidrose
Productions Ltd. for permission to
quote from *Goldfinger* on page 50.
Messrs. Wm. Heinemann Ltd.
(London), Miss Dodie Smith for
permission to quote from *Hundred
and One Dalmatians* on page 41.
Messrs. Hodder & Stoughton Ltd.,
Messrs. Charles Scribner's Sons
(New York) for permission to quote
from *Peter and Wendy* on page 28.
The Estate of Anthony Hope for
permission to quote from *Prisoner of
Zenda* on page 101. Daphne Du
Maurier, Messrs. Curtis Brown Ltd.,
Messrs. Doubleday & Co. (New York)
for permission to quote from *Rebecca*
on page 87. The Society of Authors on
behalf of the Bernard Shaw Estate for
permission to quote from *The Perfect
Wagnerite* on page 6. The Estate of
Baroness Orczy, Messrs. Hodder &
Stoughton Ltd. for permission to
quote from *The Scarlet Pimpernel* on
page 31. Messrs. John Murray Ltd.,
Messrs. Jonathan Cape Ltd.,
Baskerville Investments Ltd. for
permission to quote from *The Final
Problem* and *The Empty House* by Sir
Arthur Conan Doyle on page 82.

Illustration credits
British Library: 92, 111; William
Collins & Co: 49; *Daily Express:* 47;
John Freeman: 25, 43, 66, 73, 85, 96;
Kobal Collection: 4 (right), 21, 28,
40, 41, 44, 65, 79, 80, 95, 105; Angus
Mobean (Harvard Theatre
Collection): 87; Raymond Mander &
Joe Mitchenson Theatre Collection:
4 (left), 8, 10, 11, 13, 31, 33, 41, 72,
110, 114; Mansell Collection: 10, 82,
83, 107; National Film Archive: 5, 9,
12, 18, 24, 26, 27, 29, 32, 34, 39, 45,
46, 48, 49, 50, 51, 53, 54, 55, 56, 58,
60, 63, 67, 70, 75, 84, 89, 91, 93, 93,
97, 99, 100, 109, 113, 116, 118; Radio
Times Hulton Picture Library: 20,
22, 58, 94; Secker & Warburg: 90;
University of Cambridge Library: 7.